...ned
...ds,
...vel.

...our
...crets
...orld,
...th of
experience... ...ravel.

**Rely on Thomas Cook as your
travelling companion on your next trip
and benefit from our unique heritage.**

Thomas Cook **pocket** guides

NAPLES

Written by Ryan Levitt, updated by Petulia Melideo

Published by Thomas Cook Publishing
A division of Thomas Cook Tour Operations Limited
Company registration no. 3772199 England
The Thomas Cook Business Park, 9 Coningsby Road,
Peterborough PE3 8SB, United Kingdom
Email: books@thomascook.com, Tel: +44 (0) 1733 416477
www.thomascookpublishing.com

Produced by Cambridge Publishing Management Limited
Burr Elm Court, Main Street, Caldecote CB23 7NU
www.cambridgepm.co.uk

Series design based on an original concept by Studio 183 Limited

ISBN: 978-1-84848-412-2

© 2006, 2008 Thomas Cook Publishing
This third edition © 2011 Thomas Cook Publishing
Text © Thomas Cook Publishing
Maps © Thomas Cook Publishing/PCGraphics (UK) Limited
Transport map © Communicarta Limited

Series Editor: Karen Beaulah
Production/DTP: Steven Collins

Printed and bound in Spain by GraphyCems

Cover photography © photolibrary.com

CONTENTS

SYMBOLS KEY
The following symbols are used throughout this book:

ⓐ address ① telephone ⓦ website address ⓔ email
🕐 opening times ⓝ public transport connections ❶ important

The following symbols are used on the maps:

𝒊	information office	■	point of interest
✈	airport	◯	city
✚	hospital	◯	large town
Ⓟ	police station	○	small town
🚌	bus station	═	motorway
🚆	railway station	—	main road
Ⓜ	metro	—	minor road
✝	cathedral	—	railway
❶	numbers denote featured cafés & restaurants		

Hotels and restaurants are graded by approximate price as follows:
£ budget price ££ mid-range price £££ expensive

❍ *View of Naples and the island of Capri*

INTRODUCING
Naples

Introduction

Milan has the money, Florence the art, Venice the water and Rome the power, but Naples? Well, Naples has the heart. Gateway to the South, Naples is Italy's most spirited city. Over the centuries, countless cultures have laid claim to this glowing metropolis, yet none has held power over it for too long. It is the mighty Mount Vesuvius that forever controls the fate of this bustling port, overshadowing the region with the threat of destruction.

🔺 *The atmospheric streets of Spaccanapoli*

A visit to Naples is like a step back in time to the days when children played with sticks and balls, mothers heard and saw everything and family meals meant that entire communities shut down for Sunday dinner. Sophistication it may perhaps lack, but for a sense of 'real' Italy, you can't beat Naples.

For many years, Naples was considered a no-go area. This reputation as a crime-ridden city has largely been erased following various high-profile anti-corruption campaigns that dominated the headlines during much of the 1990s. The result is a destination that is working better than ever. Yes, there are still strikes and choking traffic problems, but a metro system is beginning to make headway and a sense of pride that hasn't been seen since before World War II is starting to creep back.

Even the UNESCO World Heritage Sites of Herculaneum (see page 102) and Pompeii (see pages 106–10) are experiencing a resurgence of interest, as debate rages on over how best to maintain the remains for the visitors of tomorrow.

Naples peaks in popularity during the summer months when it becomes the gateway to Capri (see pages 126–31), Ischia (see pages 131–5) and the Amalfi Coast (see pages 112–25). Too many travellers ignore the trappings of Naples, preferring instead to hop on the first ferry out of town. To do this is to ignore some of the finest dining possibilities, cutting-edge modern art and colourful markets in the country. Because of its charm and authenticity, Naples has become a favourite place for artists, leading to a growth in art galleries and events in the city.

Lying on the beach may top up the tan but nothing beats a Campari in the Piazza Bellini (see page 30), following a long day of church exploring. Even the splutter of the passing Vespas sounds different in this, Italy's most vibrant city.

When to go

With its Mediterranean climate, Naples is a great place to visit at any time of the year. While summer draws the bulk of the crowds, most visitors make a beeline for the islands and Amalfi Coast due to the heat and humidity, and much of the city closes down during August. Great weather and a calendar of intriguing religious and social events make May, September and October wonderful months to consider a trip. The second half of December is also particularly interesting as the whole city is buzzing with the spirit of the festive season.

SEASONS & CLIMATE

Temperatures in Naples can range from as high as 40°C (104°F) at the height of the summer, to as low as 0°C (32°F) during the bleaker months of December and January. During July and August, many

◐ Springtime at the Villa Comunale

locals head to country retreats or to family properties on Procida (see pages 135–8), Ischia (see pages 131–5) or Capri (see pages 126–31) in order to take advantage of the cooling island breezes.

Between May and September, rainfall is minimal, averaging at about 15 mm (½ in) per month. From September onwards, dampness sets in, reaching a peak in mid-November.

ANNUAL EVENTS

Neapolitans are extremely religious and superstitious, and so there are literally hundreds of events and processions in the city throughout the year. Exact dates change, so it is best to confirm dates before making any reservations. The **Azienda Autonoma di Soggiorno Cura e Turismo di Napoli** is a great resource regarding what's on. Stop by one of their three offices (see page 150), or check out their website (ⓦ www.inaples.it).

January
La Befana Festival La Befana is the Italian version of Santa Claus. She takes the form of an old hag who brings gifts to good children and leaves coal for bad ones (but the moral incentive is unclear as the lumps of 'coal' are really sweets). The distribution occurs in the Piazza del Plebiscito on 6 January.

February/March
Carnevale Naples' last chance for a party before Easter. ❶ (081) 247 1123

March
Benvenuta Primavera Uncover the secret squares and gardens of Naples during this month-long series of guided tours and theatrical happenings scattered throughout the city. ❶ (081) 247 1123

April–May

Settimana per la cultura Italy opens its famous museums free of charge for one week in the spring. Many venues extend opening hours in order to accommodate the crowds. ❶ (800) 991 199 ⓦ www.beniculturali.it

May

Galassia Gutenburg Southern Italy's largest book fair. ❸ Venue changes, check website for details ❶ (081) 230 3181 or 619 0013 ⓦ www.galassia.org

Maggio dei Monumenti Naples' largest free cultural festival offers up a vast array of events and opens some sites that have been locked for decades. ❶ (081) 247 1123 ⓦ www.comune.napoli.it

June–September

Estate a Napoli Open-air films, theatre and music all summer. ❶ (081) 247 1123 ⓦ www.napolifilmfestival.com

July

Neapolis Festival Southern Italy's largest international rock festival. Previous performers include Jamiroquai, Aerosmith and Lenny Kravitz. ⓦ www.neapolis.it

Santa Maria del Carmine The bell tower of the Santa Maria del Carmine church (❸ Piazza del Carmine 2) is 'blown up' by fireworks in a spectacular display every 15 July. The festival continues throughout the day on 16 July, with hourly Masses from 07.00 to 19.00.

August

Ferragosto The Feast of the Assumption is celebrated on 15 August. A slippery pole competition is the highlight of the festivities in Pozzuoli.

September

La festa di San Gennaro (Feast of San Gennaro) Naples' patron saint is honoured every year on 19 September (see pages 12–13).

October

Autunno Musicale A festival of classical music promoted and performed by the Nuova Orchestra Scarlatti.
Ⓦ www.nuovaorchestrascarlatti.it

December

Natale (Christmas) Nativity scenes, shoppers bustling along San Gregorio Armeno and nightly sacred music concerts.
Capodanno (New Year's Eve) Neapolitans ring in the New Year with a concert in the Piazza del Plebiscito.

PUBLIC HOLIDAYS
Capodanno (New Year's Day) 1 Jan
La Befana (Epiphany) 6 Jan
Pasqua & Lunedi di Pasqua (Easter Sunday & Monday) 7 & 8 April 2012, 30 & 31 March 2013
Festa della Liberazione (Liberation Day) 25 April
Festa del Lavoro (Labour Day) 1 May
Festa della Repubblica (Anniversary of the Republic) 2 June
Ferragosto (Feast of the Assumption) 15 Aug
Tutti Santi (All Saints' Day) 1 Nov
Festa dell'Immacolata (Feast of the Immaculate Conception) 8 Dec
Natale (Christmas) 25 Dec
Santo Stefano (Boxing Day) 26 Dec

Feast of San Gennaro

Every year on 19 September, Naples screeches to a halt as superstition, devotion and religious fervour whip city residents into a frenzy of prayer. It is on this day that the blood (sort of) of the city's patron saint, San Gennaro, liquefies (sort of) as black-clad widows and seemingly conservative residents gather together at the Duomo (for cathedral see page 76) to urge the process on. To believers, the length of time it takes for the blood to liquefy – it can be from two minutes to two hours – determines what the future year has in store, with everything from Vesuvius' eruptions to the success of the local football team blamed on the annual ritual.

San Gennaro met his end in the year 305 when he was beheaded in the *Solfatara* (sulphur mines). His blood, they say, was collected by a pious woman named Eusabia and brought to the catacombs of San Gennaro. The first incidence of the liquefaction of his blood happened a century later. Today, it can be seen bubbling on three days throughout the year: the Saturday before the first Sunday in May, the feast day itself on 19 September and on 16 December. It is only on the feast day when the future is foretold. These days, all but the most fundamentalist of Gennaro's worshippers accept that this liquefaction process is an elaborate trick (it was exposed as such in 2005), but its symbolic power is undimmed.

San Gennaro hasn't always been popular with the Vatican. During the Second Vatican Council of the 1960s, he was downgraded from saint to local cult, resulting in widespread protests and demonstrations. Pope John Paul II officially reinstated San Gennaro to his position in 1980.

To make the most of the day, arrive at the Duomo very early. The day is a national media event and brings out both celebrities and local dignitaries. A group of women called the *parenti di San Gennaro* accompany the ritual with prayers until the liquefaction is signalled by a white handkerchief.

You probably won't see the actual event close up due to the overwhelming crowds, but the visual chaos and religious splendour are sure to fascinate.

🔺 *The Duomo fills up to bursting point at the Feast of San Gennaro*

History

Naples has been an important trading post ever since it was founded by the Greeks in the 5th century BC. The Greeks were attracted by the lush soils of the region. Unfortunately, it was volcanic activity that gave the soil its nutrients.

By the 3rd century BC, Naples had been absorbed into the Roman Empire. While the region became a much-favoured playground for the rich, its status as a trade centre declined as locals were forced to build ships and supply men for the Roman navy. The eruption of Vesuvius in 79 AD was deadly, but economic depression had driven many residents away by this point. Had the volcano erupted a mere century earlier, thousands more inhabitants would have perished.

In 645 AD, the tight rein of the empire loosened. For the first time in centuries, home rule was given to a local duke and the city flourished. Attracted by booming trade and a growing arts scene, foreign invaders attacked relentlessly. Naples finally surrendered to the Norman King Roger and was absorbed into the Kingdom of Sicily in 1077. Trade once again declined and the city re-entered a period of economic depression.

Norman decline ushered in the rule of Charles of Anjou in 1256. To set him apart from his predecessors, Anjou moved the capital of the kingdom from Palermo to Naples and the city entered yet another boom time. But this period of French reign was brief, with control eventually given to the Aragonese in 1302.

For two centuries, the Aragonese ruled over a unified Southern Italy until the departure of Ferdinand III in 1502. Viceroys, despised by the local population, continued to rule *in absentia* for the next 250 years. Despite the hated leadership, Naples became Europe's largest city, with a population of 300,000 in 1600.

Between 1631 and 1656, plague and an eruption of Vesuvius killed three-quarters of the population. Following this period of destruction, residents began to rebuild in the baroque style. Many of the churches visible today can be traced back to the mid-17th century.

The Aragonese and Habsburgs continued to rule over Naples until 1860 when the region joined a unified Italy. Cholera outbreaks and mass emigration to North America depleted the population, but it was World War II that truly damaged the city's heart. Mass bombing of the ports and German destruction of the city's infrastructure forced one-third of the female population into prostitution and gave power to the Camorra mafia clans.

Today, Naples finds itself in better shape than it's been for years. Despite making the news due to waste disposal troubles linked to mismanagement by local government, corruption clean-up campaigns and financial aid from the European Union are helping the city grow in confidence. Its seductive come-hither factor increases by the day.

● *Historical relief at Castel Nuovo*

Lifestyle

The citizens of Naples are probably the most laid-back in Italy. Definitely of a 'work-to-live' mindset, they adore a good party – be it religious, cultural or just a family get-together. This relaxed attitude to life has caused other Italians to view Neapolitans as something akin to a lazy cousin – always a lot of fun but never all that motivated. But in recent years, things have changed.

Neapolitans do not seem terribly concerned with religion until the big holiday celebrations come along, though it just might be that a certain religious aspect has been seamlessly woven into the local character. However, superstition is probably more influential than religion, and you get the feeling when visiting the city that locals believe strongly in good and bad luck, with the emphasis on avoiding the latter. The most popular souvenir from the city still remains the lucky red horn, with the matchbox-sized portable saints collection not far behind. Maybe this slightly fearful approach was ingrained in the local character on account of living in the shadow of a potentially lethal volcano. The flip side of all this – and this is good news for the visitor – is a love of having a good time. Hence the friendliness of Neapolitans and the absolute importance of social contact in their lives.

Perhaps the noise generated by busy city streets explains why Neapolitan body language evolved. Whenever they need to get a point across, locals will have the precise finger wave, point, shrug or slouch ready to transmit it. As a visitor, it's probably best to regard Neapolitan sign language with the detached interest of the anthropologist – incautious attempts to deploy it when you're not fluent could result in a scene.

It would be idle to deny that the famed Camorra mafia clans that gave Naples its crime-filled reputation are still an influence, and they might impinge on the lives of some in the city. But, as a tourist, you'd have to make a determined effort to perceive even the smallest hint of their activities.

◆ *Definitely the best way to get around town*

Culture

Before the clean-up campaign that preceded the 1994 G7 summit here, the bulk of Neapolitan art could be found inside churches or under a layer of dust at the **Museo di Capodimonte** (see page 91). A resurgence in local pride has changed all that, and a boom in street and modern art has injected vibrancy into the local cultural scene. The local government is committed to funding public art; intriguing displays can be viewed at almost every metro station on the M1 line, dubbed 'Il Metro dell'Arte'.

Art lovers will rejoice in the possibility of examining gilded baroque treasures in the churches of the Centro Storico by day, and large-scale cutting-edge outdoor installations in the Piazza del Plebiscito (see page 60) as the sun sets.

Exhibition spaces at the **Castel Sant'Elmo** (see pages 88 & 90), and the **Museo Nazionale Archeologico** (see page 78) have attracted some of the biggest names in the art world. And let's not forget the incredible works of Roman art rescued from Pompeii (see pages 106–10), on show both at the Museo Nazionale Archeologico and on the site itself. **Madre-Museo d'Arte Contemporanea** (see page 63), Naples' contemporary art museum, has really enhanced the city's art profile since its opening in 2005.

If you're in the market to make a purchase, **Alfonso Artiaco** (ⓐ Piazza dei Martiri 58 ❶ (081) 497 6072 Ⓦ www.alfonsoartiaco.com Ⓝ Bus: C25), **Studio Trisorio** (ⓐ Riviera di Chiaia 215 ❶ (081) 414 306 Ⓦ www.studiotrisorio.com Ⓝ Bus: C25; tram: 1, 4) and **Galleria Raucci/Santamaria** (ⓐ Corso Amedeo di Savoia 190 ❶ (081) 744 3645 Ⓦ www.raucciesantamaria.com Ⓝ Metro: Cavour or Museo; bus: C51, C52) tend to offer the most innovative and exciting exhibitions of new work.

⬥ *The sumptuous interior of the Teatro San Carlo*

Naples loves a night at the cinema. Don't go if you are expecting a quiet night; the movies are considered a social occasion, complete with all the chattering and phone ringing that might entail, so film buffs may go slowly insane as the evening progresses. If you're feeling brave, three of the city's best cinemas are **Academy Astra** (ⓐ Via Mezzocannone 109 ⓣ (081) 552 0713 ⓦ www.astra.unina.it ⓜ Metro: Dante or Montesanto; bus: E1), **Modernissimo** (ⓐ Via Cisterna dell'Olio 23 ⓣ (081) 580 0254 ⓦ www.modernissimo.it ⓜ Metro: Dante; bus: 24, R1, R2) and **Warner Village Metropolitan Napoli** (ⓐ Via Chiaia 149 ⓣ (081) 252 5133 ⓦ www.warnervillage.it ⓜ Bus: C25; tram: 1, 4).

For theatre and opera, look no further than the **Teatro San Carlo** (ⓐ Via San Carlo 98 ⓣ (081) 797 2111 ⓦ www.teatrosancarlo.it ⓜ Bus: 24, C57, E1, R1, R2). Originally constructed in 1737, the current building is actually a replacement built in 1816 following a fire. Standards are exceptional – second only to Milan's La Scala – and tickets are consequently hard to come by. Repertoires rely mainly on traditional classics.

The Neapolitan love affair with warm weather is enhanced in the summer when outdoor music festivals offer first-class performances. The most famous celebration is the **Ravello Festival** (ⓐ Various locations, including Villa Rufolo, Ravello ⓣ (089) 858 422 ⓦ www.ravellofestival.com), which runs from June to September, depending on the year's programme. (Wagner composed sections of *Parsifal* in Villa Rufolo.) The Teatro San Carlo moves outdoors in the summer, with a rich calendar of performances taking place in the archaeological site of Baia.

◑ *The Palazzo Reale fronting on to Piazza del Plebiscito*

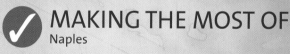 MAKING THE MOST OF
Naples

Shopping

Although Naples hasn't historically been considered a major shopping town, the local economy boom means that things are on the up.

The big designer labels – **Gucci** (🅐 Via Calabritto 4 🕐 (081) 764 0730), **Armani** (🅐 Piazza dei Martiri 61 🕐 (081) 425 816) and **Ferragamo** (🅐 Piazza dei Martiri 56 🕐 (081) 415 454) – are grouped close together, but if you want entire collections you'll need to head to Milan or Rome.

Markets inject a lot of colour into the Neapolitan shopping scene, and the biggest is **La Pignasecca**, located on the streets in and around Piazzetta Montesanto (🕐 07.00–13.00 Mon–Sat, closed Sun).

The area around Chiaia hosts famous designers as well as local artisans. Not to miss is a visit to **Marinella**, a Neapolitan tie maker famous for selling his wonderful ties to royalty and heads of government from all over the world (🅐 Riviera di Chiaia 287 🕐 (081) 764 4214). Other good, local names for custom-made bags, shoes and clothes are **Tramontano** (🅐 Via Chiaia 143 🕐 (081) 414 837 🅦 www.tramontano.it), **Eddy Monetti** (🅐 Via dei Mille 45

🔺 *Top shopping in the Galleria Umberto*

USEFUL SHOPPING PHRASES

What time do the shops open/close?
A che ora aprono/chiudono i negozi?
Ah keh ohrah ahprohnoh/kewdohnoh ee nehgotsee?

How much is this?
Quanto costa questo?
Kwantoh kostah kwestoh?

Can I try this on?
Posso provarlo?
Pohsoh prohvarloh?

My size is ...
La mia taglia è ...
Lah meeyah tahlyah eh ...

I'll take this one, thank you
Prenderò questo, grazie
Prehndehroh kwestoh, grahtsyeh

🕿 (081) 407 064 and 🏢 Piazza S Caterina 8 🕿 (081) 403 229
🌐 www.eddymonetti.it), **Finamore** (🏢 Via Recanati 27 🕿 (081) 477
602 🌐 www.finamore.it) and **Amina Rubinacci Napoli** (🏢 Via dei
Mille 16 🕿 (081) 415 672).

For something less expensive than designer labels yet more
salubrious than the market stalls, go to **Galleria Umberto** (🏢 Piazza
Trieste e Trento 🕔 24 hours) and up Via Toledo. The Galleria is a
wonderfully atmospheric covered shopping centre and Via Toledo is
the Oxford Street of Naples. Do avoid this street on Saturdays
between 18.00 and 20.00, though, as crowds can be overwhelming.

Food and drink are the best buys in Naples, thanks to the region's
culinary traditions. Almost every tourist picks up a bottle of the
city's favourite alcoholic tipple, *limoncello*. For the best stuff, wait
until you hit Capri, as this is where the drink was originally distilled.

Eating & drinking

Neapolitans love food and, although Naples is the home of pizza, there's much more to enjoy. Fresh seafood, local wine, sun-ripened produce and wonderful ice cream are just some of the treats in store. Ethnic cuisine probably isn't a realistic option: Italian food's what you'll find here, which means that meals are filling, delicious and prepared with love.

Most establishments are family-run and will have been patronised loyally by the same clientele for years. For them, it's taste rather than décor that matters, so don't be surprised if some of your best meals are in the dingiest of cafés.

Actual opening hours often vary wildly from official times, so always check ahead. Generally, though, if an eatery opens for lunch, then opening hours will be between 12.00 and 15.00. For dinner, restaurants will usually open between 19.00 and 19.30. They can close any time between 22.00 and 24.00. Most establishments are closed on a Sunday evening and one whole day in the week – usually Monday or Tuesday.

When choosing your dish, it is best to avoid ordering from the *menu turistico* as items might have been prepared earlier and frozen. Instead, opt for the *menu del giorno*. Be adventurous: some of Naples' best eateries are in the most unlikely of locations.

Many menus may be written in local dialect or feature a dish that is a speciality of the establishment. When in doubt, take a look at what other diners are tucking into and point.

PRICE CATEGORIES
Average price of a three-course meal (without drinks).
£ up to €15   ££ €15–30   £££ over €30

A LITTLE SLICE OF HEAVEN

Neapolitan chefs claim that the world's favourite fast food was invented in the wood-fired ovens of this city. Certainly, making pizza has been elevated to an art form here, and residents of various neighbourhoods have been known to battle over which pizzeria makes the best slices in town.

The best pizzerias will always have long queues snaking from their doors at all times of the day.

Traditional local choices include:

- Caprese: Fresh cherry tomatoes and mozzarella. A few leaves of *rucola* or *rughetta* (rocket) are optional.
- Capricciosa: Tomato, black olives, artichokes and ham.
- Margherita: Tomato, mozzarella, basil and oil.
- Marinara: Tomato, oregano, garlic and oil.
- Prosciutto crudo e rucola in bianco: Parma ham, mozzarella and fresh rocket.
- Ripiena: A pizza folded pastry-style stuffed with mozzarella, ricotta and salami topped with tomato and basil.
- Ripiena fritta: A deep-fried version of the Ripiena.
- Salsiccia e friarielli: Mozzarella, sausage and friarielli (a local variety of spinach).

Vegetarians shouldn't encounter any difficulties, but do be aware that southern Italians don't think of ham or bacon as meat. So, if you're uncertain, it's always a good idea to ask: *C'è la pancetta?* (Is there bacon in it?).

Italians enjoy a glass of wine with their meal. House wines are invariably local and generally very good. Between April and November,

● *Neapolitan pizza – the best in the world*

USEFUL DINING PHRASES

I would like a table for ... people
Vorrei un tavolo per ... persone
Vohray oon tahvohloh pehr ... pehrsohneh

Excuse me!	May I have the bill, please?
Scusi!	Potrei avere il conto, per favore?
Skoozhee!	*Pohtray ahveray il cohntoh, pehr fahvohreh?*

Could I have it well-cooked/medium/rare, please?
Potrei averlo ben cotto/mediamente cotto/al sangue,
per favore?
Pohtray ahvehrloh behn kohtoh/mehdyahmehnteh kohtoh/ahl sahngweh, pehr fahvohreh?

I am a vegetarian. Does this contain meat?
Sono vegetariano/vegetariana (masc/fem). Contiene carne?
Sohnoh vehjehtehrehahnoh/vehjehtehrehahnah. Kontyehneh kahrneh?

red wine is a better option as the current year's production becomes available. If you like coffee after your meal, be aware that many restaurants serve only espresso. If this doesn't sit well with you, try weaning yourself off caffeine with a shot of traditional digestive: *limoncello* (lemon flavoured), *nocillo* (made with hazelnuts) or *basilica* (basil).

Entertainment & nightlife

During the early 20th century, Naples had a reputation as a centre for Italian music. For many visitors, *la canzone napoletana* (popular song) continues to define the nation. '*O Surdato Annamurato*' and '*Funiculì, Funiculà*' are all-time favourites of this genre – but they're hardly examples of what you might call a down-with-the-kids groove.

The music and nightlife of Naples often occur on the street. Although population density is so high in this city, music venues are painfully small. Promoters, therefore, can't attract big-name acts, as sell-outs wouldn't even begin to cover their appearance fees. Instead, a good rockin' night out will require hunting for local bands, such as 24 Grana, Pino Daniele and acclaimed jazz saxophonist Daniele Sepe.

The biggest venue in Naples is **Palapartenope** (ⓐ Via Barbagallo 115 ① (081) 570 0008 ⓦ www.palapartenope.it). While perhaps not over-encumbered by atmosphere, it does occasionally bring in interesting acts and should be your first stop if live music is on your list of things to do.

During the summer months, many Neapolitans head to the hip area of Bagnoli, a former industrial area that's been reinvented into a young and lively spot.

Naples is very much a neighbourhood city, with different 'types' of people attracted to specific areas. After dark, the waterfront along Chiaia and Mergellina is very traditional. Families, the older generation and suburbanites love spending a weekend evening strolling along the bay, eating ice cream, drinking a *limoncello* (or two) and catching up on gossip. Meanwhile, Centro Storico is geared towards students, boho artists and intellectuals. These younger crowds enjoy living *La vie Bohème*: they hang out on the steps and in public squares – particularly on Piazza San

REAL TEATRO
DI S.CARLO

◓ *Try a night at the opera at the Teatro San Carlo*

Domenico Maggiore, Piazza del Gesù, Via Cisterna dell'Olio and (especially) Piazza Bellini.

During the summer, the heat makes it almost impossible to go inside any of the venues in the Centro Storico. Instead, grab a beer and walk around the streets until you find a congenial group of locals to join. This doesn't usually take long.

Locals generally leave their homes late when embarking on a night on the town. Eleven o'clock is the earliest you should even consider leaving your hotel. Midnight is even better. If you are really desperate to get inside a particular club or bar, then go when the doors open, but be prepared to be the only ones in the place for a long while.

Neapolitans are huge fans of the classics, particularly opera, and the Teatro San Carlo (see page 20) enjoys much prestige. Performances are top-notch and sell out well in advance. If you want to see anything here, purchase your ticket before arriving in the city. Please don't be tempted by touts and hawkers: many of the tickets they offer are forgeries or invalid.

Here, gaining admission to clubs is rarely a case of simply blowing a kiss to the doorman. Bars and nightclubs are generally the size of a postage stamp and admittance numbers are very limited, so negotiation and even begging may be necessary. In addition, a membership card, which you must pay for, is sometimes required. A door fee, which sometimes includes the cost of one drink, will also be charged. If you are given a card when you enter a venue, you will need to get it stamped every time you get a drink, as this is how the bar charges you at the end of the evening. Lose it and you will be subjected to a hefty fine. Do bear in mind that Neapolitans get dressed up for their nights out: if you want to have an easier time getting in, dress smartly.

◆ *Heading for a good night out in Chiaia*

Sport & relaxation

Neapolitans live and die by sport. Whether watching or playing, they put their heart and soul into it (and make sure they look good while doing so, so leave those old grey jogging bottoms at home).

SPECTATOR SPORTS

Football rules the roost, with locals devoted to the success or failure of their home team, SS Calcio Napoli. While the days of championships and Maradona are over, matches are still exciting affairs. Tickets are like gold dust but can usually be picked up from ticket sellers outside the stadium on match days. It's also worth trying the Azzurro Service box office; you never know when a pair of seats might become available.

Azzurro Service ⓐ Via F Galeota 19 ① (081) 593 4001
ⓦ www.azzurroservice.net

PARTICIPATION SPORTS

As Naples is situated on the coast, it should be no surprise that fishing and swimming are popular recreational activities. The water in Naples itself is far from clean. But you don't have to go too far to find areas suitable for a dip.

The best locations for a day's swimming are the rocky and pebbly coves on the outlying islands of Capri (see pages 126–31), Procida (see pages 135–8) and Ischia (see pages 131–5). Sorrento (see pages 122–5) and the Amalfi Coast (see pages 112–25) also have comfortable nooks where you can enjoy a dip and a spot of sunbathing. Boats based in these cleaner ports are also well placed and priced for a fishing excursion. So if you want to enjoy the sea, it's best to leave town.

If this proves inconvenient or impossible during your stay, then head in the direction of Mergellina (see page 28), where there are a few spots safe enough to risk.

RELAXATION

To relax, follow the locals to the various green spaces scattered throughout town. Jogging is extremely popular among Neapolitans. A romantic relaxation suggestion is to row your way around the bay at sunset. Not only do you get a great workout, but also you'll enjoy some of the best views of Naples. Boat rentals can be arranged on the spot just off the bridge leading to the Castel dell'Ovo.

● Football is almost a religion in Naples

Accommodation

Naples boasts just one 5-star hotel within its vibrant city centre, the Grand Hotel Parker's, with three additional havens of 5-star luxury, the Grand Hotels Vesuvio and Santa Lucia, located on Via Partenope, along the seafront, and the nearby ultra-modern Romeo Hotel. Although surprising, this isn't due to a lack of quality in the city; it's because Italy's rating system is focused around amenities rather than history, ambience or service.

For what you get, Neapolitan hotels tend to be overpriced, though summertime can bring occasional weekday deals as locals flee for cooler climes. (The exception to this rule is in the sea-facing hotels that line Via Partenope.) You'll need a bargain during your stay in Naples if you are even remotely thinking of hitting the more popular summer resorts of Ischia (see pages 131–5), Capri (see pages 126–31) or the Amalfi Coast (see pages 112–25). Room rates here can soar into the stratosphere, with 3-star properties starting at €300 per night.

Development, investment and a boom in inbound tourism due to the many low-cost flights have transformed the accommodation scene in Naples. A decade ago, the only options were crumbling 'grand dame' hotels or fleapits close to the railway station. Today, there are boutique hotels with designer accoutrements, converted *palazzi* and B&Bs oozing with character (here, the B&B is a little swisher than, say, the British version). Hotel developments are constantly being talked about, so when planning your trip keep your eyes peeled in travel news pages to see when openings occur.

HOTELS, B&BS & GUESTHOUSES
Hotel des Artistes £ A traditionally kitted-out property, close to all the main sights of the Centro Storico, slap bang in the Bohemian Quarter.

🅐 Via Duomo 61 🕕 (081) 446 155 🅦 www.hoteldesartistesnaples.it
🅝 Metro: Museo

La Locanda del Mare £ Conveniently located on the top floor of a
lovely 19th-century building, this B&B is clean and comfortable but
only has nine rooms. 🅐 Via F Caracciolo 10 🕕 (081) 195 68310
🅦 www.locandadelmare.it

Chiaia Hotel de Charme £–££ Old-fashioned class combines with
modern convenience here at what was once Naples' most chic
brothel. 🅐 Via Chiaia 216 🕕 (081) 415 555 🅦 www.hotelchiaia.it
🅝 Metro: Augusteo Via Santa Brigida

Tribu' Napoli £–££ Right in the heart of the city, this hip hotel offers
impeccable service and reasonable prices. 🅐 Via Tribunali 339
🕕 (081) 454 793 🅦 www.tribunapoli.com 🅝 Metro: Dante

B&B Chiatamone ££ A family-run B&B that's in an ideal location.
Rooms are incredibly spacious and well kept. Included in the cost of
the room is free parking nearby. 🅐 Via Chiatamone 6 🕕 (081) 060 8129
🅦 www.hotelchiatamone.it 🅝 Metro: Piazza Amedeo

Britannique ££ Originally built to cash in on the wave of British tourists embarking on 'grand tours' during the 19th century, this private villa still brings in the Brits, due to its combination of charm and elegance. ⓐ Corso Vittorio Emanuele 133 ⓣ (081) 761 4145 ⓦ www.hotelbritannique.it ⓜ Funicular: Vittorio Emanuele; bus: R2

Caravaggio Hotel di Napoli ££ This property was one of the first to be restored from dilapidated villa to chic boutique hotel. Outside is a stunning 17th-century exterior; inside is all modern light and air. ⓐ Piazza Cardinale Sisto Riario Sforza 157 ⓣ (081) 211 0066 ⓦ www.caravaggiohotel.it ⓜ Metro: Cavour

● Enjoy stunning views over the Bay of Naples

Casa Rubinacci ££ A luxury B&B owned by the well-known fashion family Rubinacci. The promise here is to experience Naples in the most stylish way, according to the famous tailor. The five suites are all named after luxury textiles and are all equally beautiful.
ⓐ Via Filangieri 26 ⓣ (081) 403 658 ⓦ www.casarubinacci.it

Parteno ££ If sea views and a Via Partenope address are what you want, but your budget doesn't agree, choose this cosy, personal hotel.
ⓐ Lungomare Partenope 1 ⓣ (081) 245 2095 ⓦ www.parteno.it
ⓝ Funicular: Mergellina; bus: R3

Micalo' ££–£££ One of Naples' few boutique hotels, Micalo' is a perfect mix of Mediterranean style and high-tech design. Its view over the bay is amazing. ⓐ Riviera di Chiaia 88
ⓣ (081) 761 7131 ⓦ www.micalo.it ⓝ Metro: Piazza Amedeo

Vesuvio ££–£££ Another celebrity favourite on the Santa Lucia seafront; indeed the luxury here has attracted everyone from Queen Victoria to Bill Clinton. ⓐ Via Partenope 45 ⓣ (081) 764 0044
ⓦ www.vesuvio.it ⓝ Funicular: Mergellina; bus: R3

Villa Capodimonte ££–£££ Looking for somewhere quiet? Then this gorgeous villa on Capodimonte hill should fit the bill.
ⓐ Salita Moiariello 66 ⓣ (081) 459 0000 ⓦ www.villacapodimonte.it
ⓝ Metro: Cavour

Excelsior £££ Politicians, jet-setters, celebrities and A-listers opt for the Excelsior as their address of choice when they're in town. Each room is unique and worth the investment. ⓐ Via Partenope 48
ⓣ (081) 764 0111 ⓦ www.excelsior.it ⓝ Metro: Piazza Amedeo

Grand Hotel Parker's £££ Staying in this luxurious hotel is like returning to the 19th century, when the hotel was the base for travellers embarking on a traditional European 'grand tour'. ❸ Corso Vittorio Emanuele 135 ❶ (081) 761 2474 ❿ www.grandhotelparkers.com ❿ Metro: Piazza Amedeo

Miramare £££ This converted Art-Deco villa that dates back to 1914 often attracts celebs, drawn by the breathtaking views over the bay. ❸ Via Nazario Sauro 24 ❶ (081) 764 7589 ❿ www.hotelmiramare.com ❿ Bus: R2

Romeo Hotel £££ A delight for architecture buffs and lovers of technology. This hotel seems a bit out of place in such an old city, but it certainly attracts a lot of interest. Two fantastic – and pricey – restaurants, and a swimming pool. ❸ Via Cristoforo Colombo 45 ❶ (081) 017 5001 ❿ www.romeohotel.it

HOSTELS & CAMPSITES

Agriturismo Il Casolare di Tobia £ A 19th-century farmhouse out west on the A56 in an extinct volcanic crater surrounded by vineyards. Its gardens and views over the fields more than make up for its distance from the city centre. ❸ Contrada Coste di Fondi Baia, Via Fabris 12, Bacoli ❶ (081) 523 5193 ❿ www.datobia.it

Averno £ This campsite is perfect if your priorities are sun and fun. It's some distance from Naples on the A56 but just 2km (1 mile) from the beach. ❸ Via Montenuovo Licola Patria 85, Pozzuoli ❶ (081) 804 2666 ❿ www.averno.it

Ostello Mergellina £ Clean, airy rooms with light-wood furniture make this hostel a popular option with backpackers. Guests can

🔺 *The elegant and upmarket Excelsior*

book either private double rooms or dormitory beds. ⓐ Salita
della Grotta 23 ① (081) 761 2346 Ⓦ www.ostellonapoli.com
Ⓝ Funicular: Mergellina; bus: R3

Vulcano Solfatara £ Just 800 m (½ mile) from the Pozzuoli metro
stop, it's a popular place for travellers on a budget. Bungalows
are also available to rent. ⓐ Via Solfatara 161 ① (081) 526 7413
Ⓦ www.solfatara.it/camping/

THE BEST OF NAPLES

Naples is an ideal destination for a short weekend break, because most of the main attractions are grouped together in either the Centro Storico or Royal Naples neighbourhoods. For day-trip suggestions, see pages 42–3.

TOP 10 ATTRACTIONS

- **Palazzo Reale** Home to the Bourbon monarchs for almost three centuries, this *palazzo* is truly stunning (see page 60).

- **Pompeii** The once-buried Roman town has become a must-see on any discerning traveller's 'grand tour' itinerary (see page 106–10).

- **Teatro San Carlo** This jewel-box of an opera house draws in the big names (see page 20).

- **Duomo** Naples' cathedral houses the remains of its patron saint, San Gennaro (see page 76). The feast day is a spectacle of prayer, wailing and miracles (see pages 12–13).

- **Museo Nazionale Archeologico** If you've been wondering where they put all the artefacts dug up from the sites at Pompeii and Herculaneum, then look no further (see page 78).

- **Piazza del Plebiscito** In this pedestrianised square you'll see the most colourful expressions of everyday Neapolitan life (see page 60).

- **Castel Sant'Elmo** This atmospheric castle has stood here since 1329. Go during one of the frequent art exhibitions when visitors are permitted to walk through the eerie interiors (see pages 88 & 90).

- **Villa Pignatelli** A charming little corner of Acton in the heart of Naples (see pages 64–5).

- **Pizza and *limoncello*** As the hometown of pizza, you'll never go wrong with a slice (see page 25) – and *limoncello* is the local contribution to the drinks cabinet (see page 23).

- **La Pignasecca** See how locals live with a visit to this massive market selling everything from leather and lace to lettuce and lemons (see page 22).

🔻 *A courtyard façade in the Palazzo Reale*

Suggested itineraries

HALF-DAY: NAPLES IN A HURRY

Stick close to the Centro Storico and Royal Naples neighbourhoods by starting your journey in the Piazza del Plebiscito (see page 60). Pop into the Museo di Palazzo Reale (see page 60) to enjoy the pomp and pageantry, followed by a quick coffee at Caffè Gambrinus (see page 70). From here, you can window-shop as you pass through the covered arcades of the Galleria Umberto (see page 23), or head directly to Via Toledo.

Quick stops inside the Gesù Nuovo (see page 76) and Santa Chiara (see page 78) churches will expose you to a little bit of Centro Storico-style religion and neighbourhood culture.

1 DAY: TIME TO SEE A LITTLE MORE

If you can spare the other half of the day, then explore the Centro Storico more fully, making sure you add the Duomo (see page 76) to the list. If time allows, pop into the Cappella Sansevero (see page 74) and admire the statue of the *Veiled Christ*. Top off the day by sipping a drink at any of the cafés on the Piazza Bellini – preferably after 24.00 when local bohemians and the student population come out to play.

2–3 DAYS: TIME TO SEE MUCH MORE

Two or three days will give you a much better impression of what the city has to offer. As well as the suggestions above, make side trips on a funicular up to Vomero (see pages 88–98) and the Castel Nuovo (see page 58). Alternatively, take a trip to the art collections and jogging trails of the Museo di Capodimonte (see page 91). A journey out of town on the Circumvesuviana railway to Pompeii (see pages 106–10) should also be slipped in.

⬤ *Take time to visit the Museo di Capodimonte*

LONGER: ENJOYING NAPLES TO THE FULL

Get more out of Naples by getting out of town. A drive along the Amalfi Coast (see pages 112–25) or a ferry journey to Capri (see pages 126–31) or Ischia (see pages 131–5) will expose you to a different side of Campanian culture and provide many lasting memories.

Something for nothing

It's easy to spend buckets of cash in a city like Naples, yet, with a little bit of planning, your stay need not be expensive. The very fact that the city's main attractions are located within a compact area means you can often dispense with public transport and walk. As the city enjoys a Mediterranean climate, a stroll along the waterfront is an enjoyable way to spend an hour or two, especially if there are public performances in the grandstand of the Villa Comunale (see pages 62–3).

There is a religious festival of some sort almost every weekend. Many of these celebrations are extremely local events, and you'll be made to feel most welcome if you join in. Thrifty culture freaks should make sure they are in town during Settimana per la cultura (see page 10) – a single week in April or May when all the museums are open to the public free of charge.

The cheapest thing to do that will expose you to 'real' Naples is to visit the city's churches. While some of the bigger places of worship charge an admission fee, most do not – and there are literally hundreds to wander through.

Not completely free, a ride on the funicular up to Vomero (see pages 88–98) is well worth the €1 expense. Not only has this inspired a famed Neapolitan song, but also it takes you up to one of the most serene districts of town. The views from the top over the Centro Storico and bay should be more than enough to reassure you.

After dark, you don't need to spend a fortune to have a good time. For something more traditional, the street-side activity along the Chiaia waterfront brings out families, black-clad grandmothers and gaggles of young couples from the suburbs. Purchase a *gelato* (ice cream) and you'll be set for the evening.

Alternatively, hang with the hipsters in the Piazza Bellini where, for the cost of an espresso, you can debate politics, admire buskers or make eyes at one of the locals as they try – possibly in vain – to seduce you from astride their Vespas.

◢ Take a free dip at one of Naples' public beaches

When it rains

The occasional shower need not spell disaster. There are more than enough churches and museums to take shelter in. If the rain looks like it's not going to stop, head to one of the bigger, indoor sights. The Museo Nazionale Archeologico (see page 78), Duomo (see page 76), Palazzo Reale (see page 60) or Museo di Capodimonte (see page 91) are the obvious possibilities. Each is big enough to keep you occupied for at least two hours.

Shopaholics will relish taking shelter in the covered arcades of the Galleria Umberto (see page 23). Or, combine architectural history with an attack on your budget by visiting the local branch of the nationwide department store La Rinascente. Located in a converted palazzo on Via Toledo, this is a beautiful shop.

In the evenings, options do become limited, especially during the summer. Neapolitans often choose rainy nights to go to the cinema, where air conditioning and gossip await. You should really only consider this option if you speak Italian.

When it rains, some places are really best avoided. If the Amalfi Coast (see pages 112–25) or Pompeii (see pages 106–10) are in your plans, think twice about visiting during a grey-weather day. The stretch of road along the Amalfi Coast is extremely treacherous even on dry days. When rain hits the tarmac, it can become a death trap. Pompeii and Herculaneum (see page 102) are no-go areas, as there is absolutely no cover anywhere on either site. Pompeii, especially, is best avoided as the streets can get extremely muddy.

The ferries and hydrofoils maintain their schedules no matter what the weather has in store. Cancellations do occur, but the storms have to be extremely strong to warrant it.

◆ *Keep out of the rain in the catacombs of San Gennaro (see pages 90–91)*

On arrival

TIME DIFFERENCE

Italian clocks follow Central European Time (CET). During Daylight Saving Time (end Mar–end Oct), the clocks are put ahead one hour.

ARRIVING

By air

Naples International Airport, otherwise known as the **Aeroporto Internazionale di Napoli Capodichino** (☎ (081) 789 6111 between 08.00 and 16.00 Mon–Fri 🔘 www.portal.gesac.it) is 8km (5 miles) from the centre of town. While it is Southern Italy's largest airport, it isn't exactly packed with facilities. Short-haul traffic makes up the bulk of flights, with the occasional charter servicing longer-haul destinations.

Getting to town from here is very easy. The journey to Stazione Centrale railway station (see below) takes 5 to 10 minutes (and it's 20 minutes to the ferry and hydrofoil ports). If you're on a budget, direct bus services make the trip to both destinations throughout the day. **Alibus** (☎ (800) 639 525 toll-free from within Italy) is the best private bus service. Its buses depart every 20 minutes from just outside the arrivals level to the Piazza Garibaldi exit of the Stazione Centrale and Piazza Municipio near the main port. Buses run from 06.30 to 23.30 and cost €3 each way.

Local buses are also a possibility. Look for the orange route 3S bus that departs every 30 minutes from outside the arrivals lounge (🕐 05.20–23.20 🔘 www.anm.it). Tickets need to be purchased in advance from the *tabacchi* (tobacconists/newsagents) inside the airport and cost €1 each way. This method should only be considered

🔺 *Save your legs and take the funicular*

if you pack light, as pickpockets target the encumbered. Don't forget to stamp your ticket once you board.

Hailing a taxi isn't a problem as there are usually dozens waiting for customers outside the arrivals area. Taxi rates between the airport and the different areas of the city have now been set at a flat fee (normally €19–20) to discourage outrageous fares. See the link on the airport's website (🆆 www.portal.gesac.it) for the most current list.

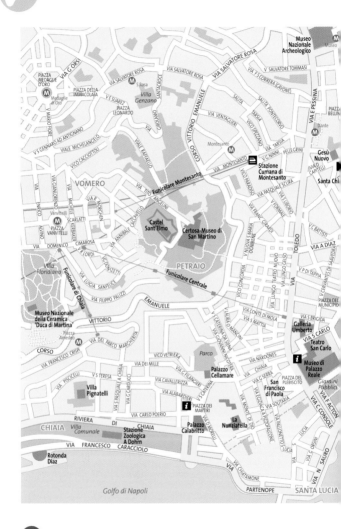

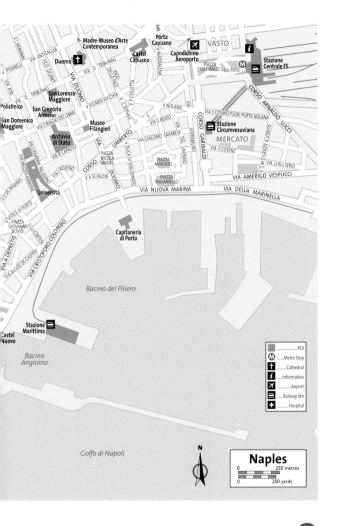

Naples

0   250 metres
0   250 yards

	POI
Ⓜ	Metro Stop
🏛	Cathedral
i	Information
✈	Airport
🚉	Railway Stn
✚	Hospital

By rail

There are three mainline stations in Naples. The one most foreign travellers arrive at is the Stazione Centrale in Piazza Garibaldi. All rapid services such as Eurostar and Intercity use this station. New bullet-train connections have made the journey time between Rome and Naples about 90 minutes.

Below street level are two lower levels. The first lower level houses the ticket counter for the Circumvesuviana line (see page 100), which services Pompeii, Herculaneum and all points to Sorrento. The second level down is Piazza Garibaldi station, used by suburban and local metro lines.

IF YOU GET LOST, TRY ...

Excuse me, do you speak English?
Mi scusi, parla inglese?
Mee scoozee, parrla eenglehzeh?

**Excuse me, is this the right way to the Old Town/
the city centre/the tourist office/the train station/
the bus station?**
Mi scusi, questa è la strada giusta per la città vecchia/
il centro/l'ufficio informazioni turistiche/la stazione
ferroviaria/la stazione degli autobus?
*Mee skoozee, kwestah eh lah strahdah justah
pehr la cheetah vehkyah/eel chentroh/loofeecho
eenfohrmahtsyonee tooreesteekah/lah stahtsyoneh
fehrohveeahreeah/lah stahtsyoneh dehlyee owtohboos?*

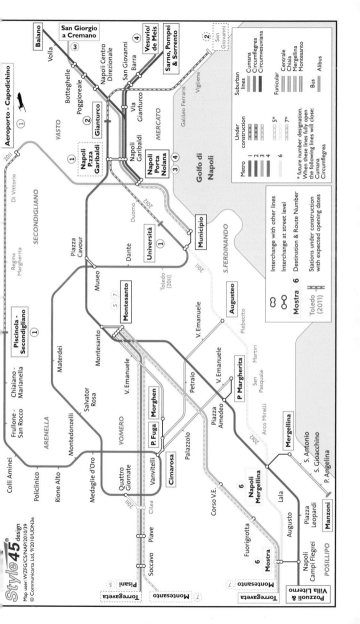

Some services also stop at Naples' other two mainline stations: Mergellina and Campi Flegrei. Check with your hotel to see if either of these stations are closer to your final destination. For all information relating to the Italian railway system, check Ⓦ www.trenitalia.it

By road

Think twice before deciding to drive to Naples. While you will need a car if you are planning a drive along the Amalfi Coast, car theft is rife, parking is impossible and city traffic is legendarily awful. If you really must bring your car, the easiest way to get here is by using Italy's motorways. From Rome and points north, take the A1 south and follow the signs to Naples. From the south and the Sorrentine Peninsula, take the A3 motorway.

By water

More and more cruise ships are including Naples on their itineraries. If you are visiting as part of a cruise, the chances are your first sight of the city will be the Molo Beverello. While not the most picturesque of corners, it's just a few steps away from the Palazzo Reale: just cross the street and turn left. It's also possible to arrive in Naples by ferry, from destinations including Corsica, Sicily and Tunisia. For further details regarding routes and timetables, check Ⓦ www.traghettitalia.it

FINDING YOUR FEET

Because central Naples is relatively compact, it doesn't take long to get the hang of the place. While pedestrianised zones are few, the size of the streets in the Centro Storico force many to walk on the cobbles. Watch out for flying Vespas. Various clean-up campaigns conducted through the 1990s have turned Naples' once-high crime statistics around. Piazza Garibaldi, the neighbourhood surrounding the railway station and the port district can still be a bit dodgy, so it is best to keep valuables hidden or back at your hotel. You'll find that a lot of younger Neapolitans speak English well, so don't be afraid to ask for any kind of help.

ORIENTATION

The streets of Naples are maze-like. The easiest way to navigate is to use Piazza del Plebiscito as a base and get your bearings from there. At the southern edge of the piazza, turn right and follow the street to the fishermen's quarter of Santa Lucia. Keep going to reach the chic shops of Chiaia.

To the north of the piazza is Via Toledo, the city's big shopping street. Formerly home to the rich and elite, their *palazzi* now house department stores and cafés. Keep going far enough on Via Toledo

△ *M is for metro*

and you'll reach the Museo Nazionale Archeologico (see page 78).
Lying even further north and on the top of a hill is Capodimonte.
You'll need to make a bus or car journey to reach the museum
that lies at the heart of this district (see page 91).

GETTING AROUND

Naples used to be difficult to get around by public transport. However,
public transportation has improved in the past years. While the city
only has two metro lines, these are supplemented by four funicular
lines that connect the lower part of the city to the higher
neighbourhoods. See ⓦ www.metro.na.it for further information.

Bus tickets must be purchased in advance. You can get them
from tobacconists (*tabacchi*) at a cost of €1 each. Once you board
the bus, don't forget to get the ticket stamped. The ticket will
then be valid for 90 minutes. Metro and funicular tickets also
cost €1 each, but can be purchased at the station.

Car hire

Driving in Naples is not advisable but you might want to hire a car
for a trip to the Amalfi Coast (see pages 112–25). The minimum age
for hiring a car is normally 25. Make sure you're covered for both
theft and collision damage.

Local and international rental companies include:

Avis ⓐ Airport ⓣ (081) 780 5790 ⓦ www.avisautonoleggio.it

Europcar ⓐ Airport ⓣ (081) 780 5643 ⓦ www.europcar.it

Hertz ⓐ Airport ⓣ (081) 780 2971 ⓦ www.hertz.it

Maggiore-Budget ⓐ Airport ⓣ (081) 780 3011 ⓦ www.maggiore.it

Thrifty ⓐ Airport ⓣ (081) 780 5702 ⓦ www.italybycar.it

◗ *The Castel Sant'Elmo sits high on a city hill*

THE CITY OF

Naples

Royal Naples & Chiaia

The Royal Naples district has been the site of Neapolitan power ever since the city was founded over 2,500 years ago. Here is where you will find the winding streets of Pallonetto's rambling fishermen's quarters, the Palazzo Reale (see page 60) and the military might of the Castel dell'Ovo (see below). Visitors interested in exploring the royal connections of the city and its history as a major Mediterranean superpower will want to make Royal Naples their home from home.

By contrast, Chiaia is a bit like the prettiest girl at school – she accepts only the best hotels, exclusive boutiques and the most fashionable of residents. Squished between the waterfront and the hills of Vomero, Chiaia stretches along the Bay of Naples until it meets the more suburban trappings of Mergellina.

SIGHTS & ATTRACTIONS

Castel Nuovo

Castel Nuovo, built in 1279 by Charles of Anjou, was given its name to distinguish it from the older Castel dell'Ovo (see below). Alterations performed in the 15th century have erased most of the original decoration. However, original Angevin architecture can still be seen in the form of the Cappella Palatina. ⓐ Piazza del Municipio ⓣ (081) 795 5877 ⓛ 09.00–19.00 Mon–Sat (ticket office closes one hour earlier), closed Sun ⓝ Bus: C25, E3, R1, R2, R3; tram: 1 ⓘ Admission charge

Castel dell'Ovo

This imposing castle is Naples' oldest, boasting a history of over 1,000 years. Built during the Norman reign, the Castel dell'Ovo was originally intended for military use, but wound up housing a monastic

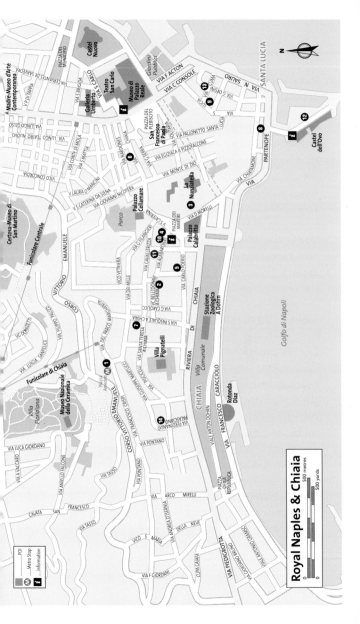

community during the Middle Ages. Many of the rooms are now offices used by the military. However, there are still plenty of sections open to the public. Be sure to climb the ramp inside the castle to reach a platform with views of the Bay below. ⓐ Borgo Marinari ⓘ (081) 240 0055 ⓗ 08.30–19.30 Mon–Sat, 09.00–13.45 Sun ⓝ Bus: 140, C24, C25, C28, R3; tram: 1

Museo di Palazzo Reale

Construction on the Royal Palace began in 1600 and took two years to complete. Then, throughout the reign of the Spanish viceroys, additions were made. The Bourbons extended the *palazzo* in the mid-18th century, while the French gave the interior its neoclassical appearance. For a building this size, it's surprising that the art collection is so poor. Instead, it's the architecture that inspires. Worth hunting for are the ornate private Teatrino di Corte theatre and the reading rooms of the Biblioteca Nazionale. ⓐ Piazza del Plebiscito ⓘ (081) 400 547 ⓗ 09.00–20.00 daily ⓝ Bus: 24, C22, C82, R2, R3 ⓘ Admission charge

Piazza del Plebiscito

Naples' largest public, pedestrianised square hosts New Year celebrations, music concerts, open-air theatre, art installations, buskers and political rallies. The surrounding Doric columns and equestrian statues dedicated to the kings of the Bourbon dynasty are popular meeting points. ⓝ Bus: 24, C22, C82, R2, R3

Stazione Zoologica A Dohrn

The Stazione Zoologica is one of Europe's oldest aquariums, having been founded in 1872. The original 30 tanks still stand, housing many regional species, including octopuses, sea horses and various

◆ The Castel dell'Ovo stands guard over the city

fish. Legend has it that the liberating forces of 1944 held a victory banquet in the aquarium that featured a menu of its entire edible population. ⓐ Viale Acquario 1, Villa Comunale ⓣ (081) 583 3111 ⓦ www.szn.it ⓛ 09.00–18.00 Tues–Sat, 09.30–19.30 Sun, closed Mon (Mar–Oct); 09.00–17.00 Tues–Sat, 09.00–14.30 Sun, closed Mon (Nov–Feb) ⓝ Bus: 140, 152, C9, C10, R3; tram: 1

Villa Comunale

This park, designed by Luigi Vanvitelli in 1781, was originally reserved strictly for royalty. Today, it is the city's most well-loved stretch of greenery. A bandstand, built in 1867, occasionally hosts

⬤ *San Francesco di Paola in the elegant Piazza del Plebiscito*

public concerts and performances. ⓐ Riviera di Chiaia ⓛ 07.00–24.00 daily, May–Oct; 07.00–22.00 Nov–Apr ⓝ Bus: 140, 152, C28, R3; tram: 1

CULTURE

Madre-Museo d'Arte Contemporanea

Hosted in the beautiful Palazzo Donna Regina, this gallery provides a welcome break from ancient art. The permanent collection and temporary exhibits are of international standard, but its future is uncertain due to lack of funds. ⓐ Via Settembrini 79 ⓣ (081) 1931 3016 ⓦ www.museomadre.it ⓛ 10.00–19.00 Wed–Mon, closed Tues ⓝ Bus: C24, C25, C28 ⓘ Admission charge; free on Mon

La Nunziatella

Built for the Bourbons in 1787, this tiny church features a beautiful marble altar and unique tile flooring. Today, it is owned and used by the military academy located next door. ❸ Via Generale Parisi 16 🕓 09.00–10.00 Sun for Mass; all other times by appointment only Ⓝ Bus: 140, C24, C25, C28, R3; tram: 1

San Francesco di Paola

Naples has a lot of churches, but very few of them were built in the neoclassical style. San Francesco di Paola is the major exception – and is not much liked by locals for this reason. The church is a simple yet majestic imitation of Rome's Pantheon, often marred by political graffiti. ❸ Piazza del Plebiscito ❶ (081) 764 5133 Ⓦ www.basilicaplebiscito.it 🕓 08.00–12.00, 15.30–17.00 Mon–Sat, 08.00–13.00 Sun Ⓝ Bus: 24, C22, C82, R2, R3

Villa Pignatelli

Ferdinand Acton, son of the former British prime minister Sir John Acton, built this villa in the 19th century, complete with

MARKETS

The Bancarelle di San Pasquale and the Fiera Antiquaria Napoletana are both great markets. Located between Via San Pasquale and Via Carducci, the Bancarelle sells a wide selection of food, spices, fish, clothing and inexpensive jewellery on Mondays, Wednesdays, Fridays and Saturdays. The Fiera Antiquaria Napoletana is held much less frequently, on the last Sunday of the month, excluding August. Sellers set up along the Riviera di Chiaia, offering furniture, paintings, porcelain and jewellery.

an English-style garden. The Italian government took it over in 1952 and it now showcases a collection of porcelain figurines and busts. Landscape paintings are also in abundance. ⓐ Riviera di Chiaia 200 ⓣ (081) 761 2356 ⓛ 08.30–13.30 Wed–Mon, closed Tues ⓦ Bus: 140, 152, C28, R3 ⓘ Admission charge

RETAIL THERAPY

The main shopping streets can all be found in Chiaia, as most of the boutiques in Royal Naples are heavily geared towards tourist tat. The exception to this is Galleria Umberto (see page 23). This covered shopping centre may remind some visitors of the Galleria in Milan.

Amina Rubinacci Ms Rubinacci set up her Neapolitan fashion house in the 1970s and since then she's become an icon of style and quality. The knitwear here is incredible. ⓐ Via dei Mille 16 ⓣ (081) 415 672 ⓦ www.aminarubinacci.it ⓛ 10.00–13.30, 16.30–20.00 Mon–Sat, closed Sun ⓦ Funicular: Chiaia to Parco Margherita; metro: Piazza Amedeo; bus: C25

La Bottega della Ceramica Beautiful handmade ceramics collected from across southern Italy. Prices are very reasonable. ⓐ Via Carlo Poerio 40 ⓣ (081) 764 2626 ⓛ 10.00–13.30, 16.30–20.00 Mon–Sat, closed Sun ⓦ Bus: C25; tram: 1, 4

Eddy Monetti This is truly classic Italian clothing. Considered the ultimate in quality, the style is conservative yet timeless. A true institution. Men: ⓐ Via dei Mille 45 ⓣ (081) 407 064 ⓦ www.eddy monetti.com ⓦ Funicular: Chiaia to Parco Margherita; metro: Piazza Amedeo; bus: C25. Women: ⓐ Piazzetta Santa Caterina 8, off Piazza

⬥ The Galleria Umberto is a beautiful place to shop

dei Martiri ☏ (081) 403 229 🕐 09.30–13.30, 16.30–20.00 Mon–Sat, closed Sun, Mon mornings in winter & two weeks Aug (Men & Women) Ⓝ Bus: C25; tram: 1, 4

Gay Odin The oldest chocolate shop in Naples, here you can buy – or indulge in – all varieties of cocoa-based delights. ⓐ Via Vetriera 12 ☏ (081) 417 843 Ⓦ www.gayodin.it 🕐 08.30–17.00 Mon–Sat, closed Sun Ⓝ Metro: Piazza Amedeo

Marinella Top ties and accessories for the man who has everything. ⓐ Riviera di Chiaia 287A ☏ (081) 764 4214 Ⓦ www.marinellanapoli.it 🕐 07.00–13.00, 15.30–20.00 Mon–Sat, closed Sun & two weeks Aug Ⓝ Bus: C28; tram: 1, 4

Maxi Ho Fashion-forward designer duds from the likes of Prada and Dolce & Gabbana. ⓐ Via Nisco 24 ☏ (081) 410 231 🕐 09.30–13.00, 16.30–20.00 Mon–Sat, closed Sun & one week Aug Ⓝ Funicular: Chiaia to Parco Margherita; metro: Piazza Amedeo; bus: C25

De Nobili Exclusive decorative pieces in gold, coral and precious stone, which can be commissioned according to individual specifications. ⓐ Via Filangieri 16 ☏ (081) 421 685 Ⓦ www.denobili.com 🕐 10.00–13.30, 16.30–20.00 Mon–Sat, closed Sun Ⓝ Bus: C25; tram: 1, 4

Outlet Fashion This huge store offers designer clothes at discounted prices. Definitely worth a visit for bargain hunters. ⓐ Via Vittoria Colonna 14b, 32 🕐 10.00–13.30, 16.30–20.00 Mon–Sat, closed Sun & Aug Ⓝ Tram: 1, 4

Penna & Carta 1989 When was the last time you wrote a letter? Be inspired by the handmade stationery and glass pens. ⓐ Largo Vasto a Chiaia 86 ❶ (081) 418 724 ⓦ www.pecnapoli.com ❶ 10.00–13.30 Tues–Sat, 16.30–20.00 Mon–Sat, closed Sun & Aug ❶ Bus: C25; tram: 1, 4

Siola High-end, designer maternity and childrenswear purveyor. Labels include Armani and Pinko Pallino. ⓐ Via Chiaia 113 ❶ (081) 415 036 ⓦ www.siola.it ❶ 10.00–13.30, 16.30–20.00 Mon–Sat, closed Sun; also closed Sat afternoons (summer), Mon mornings (winter) & two weeks Aug ❶ Bus: C25; tram: 1, 4

TAKING A BREAK

Caffè Amadeus £ ❶ The large number of outside tables is the main draw of this café. ⓐ Piazza Amedeo 5 ❶ (081) 761 3023 ❶ 07.00–03.00 daily ❶ Metro: Piazza Amedeo; bus: C24, C25

La Focaccia 'Eating in Naples' £ ❷ Choose from an incredible selection of pizza slices and *focaccia* if you fancy a quick nibble. ⓐ Vico Belledonne a Chiaia 31 ❶ (081) 412 277 ❶ 10.00–02.00 Mon–Sat, 18.00–03.00 Sun, closed three weeks Aug ❶ Bus: C22, C25

Vinarium £ ❸ For a leisurely glass of wine and a snack, Vinarium is great. Be prepared to queue at weekends. ⓐ Vico Santa Maria Cappella Vecchia 7 ❶ (081) 764 4114 ❶ 11.00–16.30, 19.00–01.30 Mon–Sat (Sept–June); 12.00–16.00 Mon–Sat (July); closed Sun & Aug

La Caffettiera £–££ ❹ An elegant café that's popular for its inspiring interior and old-fashioned service. ⓐ Piazza dei Martiri 26 ❶ (081) 764

◆ The Neptune fountain in Via Medina

4243 Ⓦ www.grancaffelacaffettiera.com Ⓛ 08.00–21.30 Mon–Fri, 08.00–22.00 Sat & Sun, closed two weeks Aug Ⓝ Bus: C25

Anelho ££ ❺ Located in a former film theatre, this café/restaurant is open daily from morning until night and it's ideal for a light snack. Ⓐ Via Carlo Poerio 47 Ⓣ (081) 764 5764

Caffè Gambrinus £££ ❻ The revolutionaries and poets are long gone but it's easy to see why Gambrinus remains the most popular café in Naples: location, location, location. Ⓐ Via Chiaia 1–2 Ⓣ (081) 417 582 Ⓦ www.caffegambrinus.com Ⓛ 08.00–01.30 daily Ⓝ Funicular: Centrale to Augusteo; bus: 24, C22, C25, C57

AFTER DARK

RESTAURANTS

Osteria da Tonino £–££ ❼ A laid-back *osteria* that offers tasty dishes on a budget. A great place to go for a relaxed, flavoursome meal. Ⓐ Via Santa Teresa a Chiaia 47 Ⓣ (081) 421 533 Ⓛ lunch 12.30–16.00 daily; dinner 19.30–01.00 Wed–Sun Ⓝ Funicular: Chiaia to Parco Margherita; metro: Piazza Amedeo; bus: C24, C25, C26, C27, C28

Ciro ££ ❽ Located almost at the base of the Castel dell'Ovo, it's a delightful eatery from which to enjoy the sunset over the Bay. Ⓐ Via Luculliana 29–30 Ⓣ (081) 764 6006 Ⓦ www.ristoranteciro.it Ⓛ 12.30–15.30, 19.30–24.00 Mon & Tues, Thur–Sun, closed Wed Ⓝ Bus: C25

Osteria degli Antichi Sapori ££ ❾ A former grocery store that's evolved into a lively, reasonably priced restaurant. Ⓐ Via Santa

Lucia 16 ❶ (081) 245 1183 ❷ 12.00–16.00, 20.00–24.00 Mon–Sat, closed Sun ❷ Bus: 25

La Stanza del Gusto ££ ❿ Located just off the busy Via Chiaia, this lovely find serves a menu of seasonal dishes that changes every day. ❸ Via Constantinopoli 100 ❶ (081) 401 578 ❷ 10.30–24.00 Mon–Sat, closed Sun & three weeks July & Aug ❷ Bus: 140, C9, C18, C22, C25

Umberto ££ ⓫ The only vegetarian restaurant in town worth mentioning. The food is flavoursome, and gluten-free dishes are also available. ❸ Via Alabardieri 30 ❶ (081) 418 555 ❿ www.umberto.it ❷ 12.00–16.00, 19.00–23.00 Tues–Sun, closed Mon & three weeks Aug ❷ Metro: Piazza Amedeo; bus: C25, R3

Zi Teresa ££ ⓬ A family-run eatery that's been dishing out delicious seafood since 1890. Tables overlooking the port are the most coveted. ❸ Borgo Marinaro 1 ❶ (081) 764 2565 ❷ 12.30–15.30, 20.00–23.30 Tues–Sat, 12.30–16.00 Sun, closed Mon & Aug ❷ Bus: C25

La Cantinella £££ ⓭ This is the restaurant Neapolitans choose for special occasions. The quality of the seafood is uniformly excellent. Service is first class, the settting is formal: jacket and tie required. ❸ Via Cuma 42 ❶ (081) 764 8684 ❿ www.lacantinella.it ❷ 12.30–15.00, 19.30–23.30 Mon–Sat, closed Sun & two weeks Aug ❷ Bus: C25

Da Dora £££ ⓮ If you're going to splurge, then do it here. This tiny restaurant offers the best fish in town. ❸ Via Ferdinando

Palasciano 30 ☎ (081) 680 519 🕐 12.30–15.00, 20.00–24.00
Mon–Sat, closed Sun & three weeks Aug Ⓜ Bus: 140, C9, C18,
C24, C25, C28

BARS, CLUBS & DISCOS

Culti Spa Café Cool factor ten! This is a concept bar, where you can
get your morning coffee or your martini, then a Thai massage or
a manicure. ⓐ Via Carlo Poerio 47 ☎ (081) 764 4919 🕐 10.00–22.00
daily Ⓜ Metro: Piazza Amedeo; bus: C25, R3

Enoteca Belledonne This minuscule bar gets packed, and if you find
crowds difficult, don't even think about going any time between
19.00 and 21.00. ⓐ Vico Belledonne a Chiaia 18 ☎ (081) 403 162
Ⓦ www.enotecabelledonne.com 🕐 09.00–14.00 Mon–Sat,
16.30–22.00 Mon–Thur, 16.30–02.00 Fri & Sat, closed Sun & Aug
Ⓜ Metro: Piazza Amedeo; bus: C25, R3

Farinella A New York-style loft that's perfect for a drink after
dinner or just for a relaxed night. The bar gets crowded quickly.
ⓐ Via Alabardieri 10 ☎ (081) 423 8455 🕐 19.00–02.00 Tues–Sat,
19.00–03.00 Sun, closed Mon & Aug Ⓜ Metro: Piazza Amedeo;
bus: C25, R3

Marshall Lounge For lovers of minimalist chic, this tiny bar
should be on your must-sip list. ⓐ Vico Belledonne a Chiaia 12
☎ (081) 405 216 🕐 18.00–02.00 Tues–Sun, closed Mon & July–Sept
Ⓜ Metro: Piazza Amedeo; bus: C25, R3

Otto Jazz A local haunt that attracts fans of traditional jazz.
Performers come from the surrounding regions and, boy, do they

blow hot. @ Salita Cariati 23 ❶ (081) 551 3765 ❶ 23.00–02.00 Sun–Fri, closed Sat & Aug Ⓝ Funicular: Centrale to Corso Vittorio Emanuele; bus: C16

CINEMAS & THEATRES

Amedeo Small space that shows films in English on Thursdays. @ Via Martucci 69 ❶ (081) 680 266 Ⓝ Metro: Piazza Amedeo; bus: C24, C25

Mercadente Naples' main theatrical performance space has been in existence since 1779. Some of Italy's best-known actors can often be found here treading the boards. @ Piazza del Municipio 1 ❶ (081) 551 336 Ⓦ www.teatrostabilenapoli.it Ⓝ Bus: 24, C22, C25, C57

Politeama Performance space in a former monastery that often hosts modern dance and live music. @ Via Monte di Dio 80 ❶ (081) 764 5001 Ⓦ www.teatropoliteamanapoli.com ❶ Box office: 10.00–13.00, 16.30–18.30 Mon–Sat, closed Sun (Oct–May) on performance days Ⓝ Bus: C22

Villa Pignatelli This luxurious villa showcases double bills that combine old and new, and well-known with rare. Most films are screened in their original language. @ Riviera di Chiaia 200 ❶ (081) 425 037 Ⓦ www.galleriatoledo.org Ⓝ Bus: C28, R3

Centro Storico & La Sanità

For many years, the city of Naples was just the Centro Storico. Bound by the city walls, thousands of residents packed into its tight, winding streets to live in what was at one time the most populated city on the planet. These winding streets remain, giving the area its strong neighbourhood character – especially in Spaccanapoli, the collection of pedestrianised, laundry-clad streets that slices the area in two.

If you have just one day to spend in Naples, then this is the district to explore. Packed with churches, archaeological sites and one of Naples' most renowned museums, it's a living history and anthropology lesson – but a lot more fun than any lecture.

SIGHTS & ATTRACTIONS

Cappella Sansevero

The funerary chapel of the Di Sangro family is known best for the beautiful statue of the veiled Christ and the macabre figures in the crypt. Legend has it that they are the dead bodies of the family's domestic staff. ⓐ Via Francesco de Sanctis 19 ⓣ (081) 551 8470 ⓦ www.museosansevero.it ⓛ 10.00–17.40 Mon, Wed–Sat, 10.00–13.10 Sun, closed Tues ⓜ Metro: Dante or Montesanto; bus: E1 ⓘ Admission charge

Catacombe di San Gaudioso

This extensive subterranean collection of catacombs holds the remains of St Gaudiosus, a 5th-century North African bishop. His burial here has transformed the labyrinthine cave system into an important shrine and place of holy pilgrimage. Fans of the macabre will appreciate

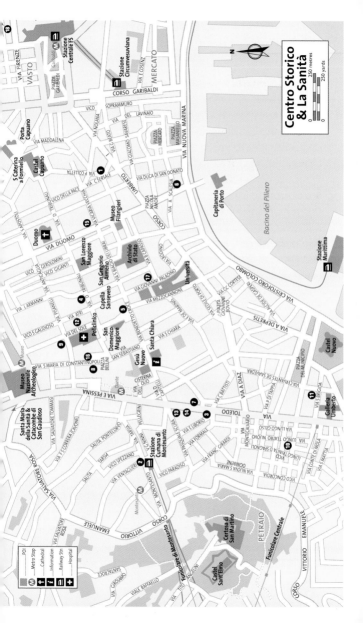

Centro Storico & La Sanità

0 — 350 metres
0 — 250 yards

N

Stazione Centrale FS

Stazione Circumvesuviana

CORSO GARIBALDI

MERCATO

VIA FIRENZE

VASTO

PIAZZA GARIBALDI

VICO SOPRAMMURO

VIA NOLANA

VICO DEL LAVINAIO

VIA MADDALENA

Porta Capuano

S Caterina a Formiello

Castel Capuano

VIA TRIBUNALI VECCHIA

VIA S BROSOLO

VICO ANTICAGLIA

VICO GIGANTI

VICO CEROLOMINI

Duomo

VIA DUOMO

VIA COLLETTA

VIA A TREVICO

VICOLO DELLA PACE

CORSO UMBERTO I

VIA CESERCALE

Museo Filangeri

San Lorenzo Maggiore

San Gregorio Armeno

DELL'ARMA

Archivio di Stato

VIA CARBONARA

VIA GIACOMO SAVARESE

PIAZZA NICOLA AMORE

VIA A SCALA

VIA DUCA DI SAN DONATO

PIAZZA MERCATO

PIAZZA MASANIELLO

VIA NUOVA MARINA

Capitaneria di Porto

Bacino del Piliero

Stazione Marittima

VIA CRISTOFORO COLOMBO

VIA A DEPRETIS

VIA CORSEA

VIA S MARIA DI CONSTANTINOPOLI

Museo Nazionale Archeologico

VIA S MARIA DELLE GRAZIE

Santa Maria delle Anime & Catacombe di San Gaudioso

VIA SALVATORE ROSA

VIA SALVATORE TOMMASI

VIA CONFORTO CAIONE

SALITA PONTECORVO

TARSIA

VICO SPEZZANO

PIAZZA BELLINI

VIA CISTERNA DELL'OLIO

Gesù Nuovo

Santa Chiara

VIA S SEBASTIANO

San Domenico Maggiore

Cappella Sansevero

Polifclinico

VIA DEL SOLE

VIA ATRI

VICO S GAUDIOSO

VIA PESSINA

VIA F S CORRERA

VIA PELLEGRINI

VICO LUNGO TRINITÀ DEGLI SPAGNOLI

VICO LUNGO TEATRO NUOVO

Università

VIA GIOVANNI PALADINO

VIA MEZZOCANNONE

VIA PORTO

VIA SEDILE DI PORTO

PIAZZA GIOVANNI BOVIO

VIA CC CORTESE

VIA A DIAZ

PIAZZA DEL MUNICIPIO

Castel Nuovo

VIA CERVANTES DE SAAVEDRA

VIA G BRUNO

VIA TOLEDO

Galleria Umberto

VIA S BRIGIDA

Certosa di San Martino

Castel Sant'Elmo

Funicolare Centrale

PETRAIO

CORSO VITTORIO EMANUELE

VIALE RAFFAELLO

VIA TITO ANGELINI

Funicolare di Montesanto

Stazione Cumana di Montesanto

CORSO VITTORIO EMANUELE

SALITA SANTA CROCE

VIA SALVATORE ROSA

Legend:
- POI
- Metro Stop
- Information
- Cathedral
- Railway Stn
- Hospital

the displays chronicling ancient burial practices. Tours depart
from the church of the Santa Maria della Sanità across the street.
ⓐ Via Sanità 124 ⓣ (081) 544 1305 ⓦ www.catacombedinapoli.it
ⓛ Church: 08.30–12.30, 17.00–20.00 Mon–Sat, 08.30–13.30 Sun;
catacombs: guided tours 10.00, 11.00, 12.00, 13.00 ⓜ Metro: Piazza
Cavour or Museo; bus: C51, C52 ⓘ Admission charge

Duomo

Housing the remains of Naples' patron saint San Gennaro, the Duomo
is the most important church in the city. Its history can be dated
back to the 4th century, but the structure that stands today was built
in the 13th century over the remains of two previous houses of worship.
ⓐ Via Duomo 147 ⓣ (081) 449 097 ⓦ www.duomodinapoli.com
ⓛ Cathedral: 08.00–12.30, 16.30–19.00 Mon–Sat, 08.00–13.30,
17.00–19.30 Sun; archaeological area & baptistery: 09.00–12.00,
16.30–19.00 Mon–Sat, 09.00–12.30 Sun ⓜ Bus: E1, R2

Gesù Nuovo

Originally a *palazzo*, this church is notable for its façade of raised,
diamond-shaped stone. The interiors were transformed from a place
of worship in the 16th century. Of particular interest is the room
dedicated to local saint Giuseppe Moscati, a 20th-century Neapolitan
doctor who forsook the trappings of wealth and prestige in order
to tend to the health of the local poor. ⓐ Piazza del Gesù Nuovo 2
ⓣ (081) 551 8613 ⓛ 06.45–13.00, 16.00–19.30 daily ⓜ Metro:
Montesanto or Dante; bus: E1, R1

San Lorenzo Maggiore

Take a trip back in time to Graeco-Roman Neapolis and wander the
ancient streets of Naples discovered under the church, in what is truly

the most wondrous ancient site in the city. Excavation work is ongoing, but a butcher's shop, bakery, dyer's stall and porticoed arcade are all accessible. ⓐ Via dei Tribunali 316 ⓣ (081) 211 0860 ⓦ www.sanlorenzomaggiorenapoli.it ⓛ 09.30–17.30 Mon–Sat, 09.30–13.30 Sun ⓜ Metro: Dante or Montesanto; bus: E1 ⓘ Admission charge

⬤ The Duomo is Naples' most important church

Santa Chiara

This Gothic church was built during the reign of Robert of Anjou.
World War II bombs and Baroque-era reconstruction have done much
to reduce this place of worship – after the war, all that was left were
the four walls. The cloister contains pieces from the original 14th-
century structure and shards of shrapnel. ⓐ Via Santa Chiara 49
ⓣ (081) 552 6280 ⓛ Church: 08.00–12.30, 16.30–19.30 daily; museum
& cloister: 09.30–13.00, 14.30–17.30 Mon–Sat, 09.30–13.00 Sun
ⓜ Metro: Dante or Montesanto; bus: E1

CULTURE

Museo Nazionale Archeologico

This former *palazzo* that once housed Naples University was
converted by King Ferdinand I into a private art gallery after he
inherited hundreds of ancient pieces from his grandmother.

Following the discovery of the ruins at Pompeii, the rooms
quickly filled up. Boasting one of the most important collections
of Roman antiquities in the world, the Museo Nazionale is truly
the crown jewel of all the museums in the city. The bulk of the
treasures taken from Herculaneum and Pompeii can be found on
the first floor centred on the Sala Meridiana.

The museum also hosts some remarkable pieces of the
Farnese Collection. Attempts to attract younger visitors have
resulted in a number of temporary exhibits in the rooms off
the main courtyard. Recent artists profiled include Jeff Koons
and Damien Hirst. ⓐ Piazza Museo 19 ⓣ (081) 292 823
ⓦ http://museoarcheologiconazionale.campaniabeniculturali.it
ⓛ Museum: 09.00–19.30 Mon & Wed–Sun, closed Tues ⓜ Metro:
Piazza Cavour or Museo; bus: 47, CS, E1 ⓘ Admission charge

A WALK THROUGH THE CENTRO STORICO

Begin your walk by exploring the Duomo (see page 76),
home to Naples' patron saint, Gennaro, and certainly the
city's most important ecclesiastical building. Although this
particular structure was built in the 13th century, a church
of some sort has been sitting on the site since the 4th century.
Turn left out of the Duomo and walk down Via Duomo, then
turn right where it intersects with Via dei Tribunali. Follow
the latter and, a few steps along on your left, you'll soon see
San Lorenzo Maggiore (see pages 76–7), a church that
regularly produces miracles in the shape of archaeological
treasures that will connect you directly to the city's ancient
past. Continue along Via dei Tribunali until you get to Cappella
Sansevero (see page 74), with its stunning statue of Christ and
sombre funerary figures. When you rejoin Via dei Tribunali, on
your left you'll see yet another church, San Domenico
Maggiore. If all that religious majesty leaves you feeling
maybe a touch too awe-inspired, come back down to earth
with a coffee and a chat among the friendly café-culture
vultures of Piazza Bellini (see page 30).

RETAIL THERAPY

For many, the highlight of a visit to the Centro Storico and La Sanità
is the shopping. The street scenes and service draw people in, as each
boutique has quirky characteristics that make shopping fun. The high-
street shops of Via Toledo are in converted *palazzi* that were once owned
by the wealthy. Their exteriors alone are worth a spot of browsing.

● *Beautiful Santa Chiara*

Antiche Delizie Foodies will love the mouthwatering selection of mozzarellas, antipasti, truffles and cured meats. Service is very friendly. ❸ Via Pasquale Scura 14 ● 08.00–20.00 Mon–Wed, Fri & Sat, 08.00–15.00 Thur, 09.00–14.00 Sun, closed one week Aug Ⓜ Metro: Montesanto; bus: 24, 105, R1

Enoteca Dante Family-owned wine shop that sells both local and imported varieties. ❸ Piazza Dante 18 ❶ (081) 549 9689

🕐 09.00–20.30 Mon–Sat, closed Sun & two weeks Aug
Ⓜ Metro: Dante or Montesanto; bus: 24, 105, R1

Evaluna Bookshop A centre of cultural activities, book presentations and art shows, Evaluna is much more than a (very fine) bookshop.
🅐 Piazza Bellini 72 🕐 (081) 292 372 🕐 19.30–24.00 Mon, 10.00–14.00 Tues–Sat, closed Sun Ⓦ www.evaluna.it Ⓜ Metro: Dante

Garlic Not for the fashion faint-hearted, Garlic showcases the new, the adventurous and the just plain wild. 🅐 Via Toledo 111
🕐 (081) 5524 4966 🕐 10.00–20.00 Mon–Sat, closed Sun & two weeks Aug Ⓜ Metro: Montesanto; bus: 24, 105, R1

Gioielleria Leonardo Gaito A jewellery shop that offers classic pieces in gold and silver. Definitely the place to go for something special. 🅐 Via Toledo 278 🕐 (081) 421 104 🕐 10.00–19.30 Mon–Sat, closed Sun & three weeks Aug Ⓜ Funicular: Centrale to Augusteo; bus: R1, R2, R4

Marco Ferrigno Many people come to Naples purely with the intention of purchasing Nativity figurines. When you see the terracotta offerings at this cave-like boutique, you will understand why. Highly collectable. 🅐 Via San Gregorio Armeno 8 🕐 (081) 552 3148 Ⓦ www.arteferrigno.it 🕐 09.30–13.30, 16.00–20.00 Mon–Sat, closed Sun & three weeks Aug Ⓜ Bus: E1

Napoli Mania For souvenirs that are a step up from the usual tat, head to this witty boutique in the heart of Via Toledo. 🅐 Via Toledo 312 🕐 (081) 613 3221 Ⓦ www.napolimania.com 🕐 10.00–13.45, 16.30–20.00 daily Ⓜ Funicular: Centrale to Augusteo; bus: C25, R2

Talarico Naples' oldest handicraft shop, specialising in umbrellas. The owners pride themselves on keeping the skills of local craftspeople and artisans alive. ➌ Vico Due Porte a Toledo 4B ➊ (081) 401 979 Ⓦ www.mariotalarico.it ⓛ 09.30–20.00 Mon–Sat, closed Sun & Aug Ⓝ Bus: C28; tram: 1, 4

TAKING A BREAK

Antica Pizzeria da Michele a Forcella £ ❶ This just might be the best pizza place in town. They only make two kinds: *marinara* (red sauce) and *margherita* (red sauce and cheese), according to the true tradition and philosophy of pizza-making. ➌ Via Cesare Sersale 1/3 ➊ (081) 553 9204 ⓛ 10.00–23.00 Mon–Sat, closed Sun Ⓝ Metro: Garibaldi

Friggitoria Firoenzano £ ❷ Tasty snacks that make a change from the usual slices of pizza. When in season, the deep-fried artichokes are heavenly. ➌ Piazza Montesanto 6 ⓛ 08.00–22.00 Mon–Sat, closed Sun & two weeks Aug Ⓝ Metro: Montesanto

Gelateria della Scimmia £ ❸ Naples' oldest and most established *gelateria*. ➌ Piazza Carità 4 ➊ (081) 552 0272 Ⓦ www.gelateriadellascimmia.it ⓛ 10.00–24.00 Mon, Tues, Thur & Fri, 10.00–01.00 Sat & Sun, closed Wed Ⓝ Funicular: Centrale to Augusteo; metro: Montesanto; bus: R1, E3

Di Matteo £ ❹ The décor at this pizzeria is nothing to write home about; the slices, on the other hand, are. ➌ Via dei Tribunali 94 ➊ (081) 455 262 Ⓦ www.pizzeriadimatteo.it ⓛ 10.00–24.00 Mon–Sat, closed Sun & two weeks Aug Ⓝ Metro: Dante; bus: R1, R2

Scaturchio £–££ ❺ Here you will find the original recipe of the *ministeriale*, a delicious mix of chocolate, liquor and coffee in the shape of a large coin. ⓐ Piazza San Domenico Maggiore 19 ⓣ (081) 551 6944 ⓦ www.scaturchio.it ⓛ 08.00–24.00 daily ⓜ Metro: Museo or Piazza Cavour; bus: CS, E1, R2

Antica Osteria del Borgo ££ ❻ Family-run *osteria* serving the traditional Neapolitan dishes. A favourite among locals but note that it's only open at lunchtime. ⓐ Via Carlo Troja 34 ⓣ (081) 204 745

La Chiacchierata ££ ❼ This tiny eatery exudes Neapolitan spirit. The food's impeccable, tasty and traditional, and the hosts are fun. Make sure you try the unbelievable *gnocchi*. ⓐ Piazzetta Matilde Serao 37 ⓣ (081) 411 1465 ⓛ 12.00–14.00 daily ⓜ Metro: Augusteo

AFTER DARK

RESTAURANTS

Caffè Intra Moenia £ ❽ A literary salon where the intelligentsia of Naples gather for talks, poetry readings and spectacular pasta. ⓐ Piazza Bellini 70 ⓣ (081) 451 652 ⓦ www.intramoenia.it ⓛ 09.00–01.00 daily ⓜ Metro: Dante

Cantina della Sapienza £ ❾ If you don't get an invitation to a Neapolitan home for a meal, then a stop at the Cantina della Sapienza is the next best thing. The menu offers both intriguing original dishes and local favourites. ⓐ Via della Sapienza 40 ⓣ (081) 459 078 ⓛ 12.00–15.30 Mon–Sat, closed Sun & three weeks Aug ⓜ Metro: Piazza Cavour; bus: C57, R4

Cantina della Tofa £ ❿ The menu reflects Neapolitan traditions. From the pasta with shrimp and zucchini to the braised beef, everything is good and very affordable. ❸ Vico della Tofa 71 ❶ (081) 406 840 Ⓦ www.cantinadellatofa.com ❶ 12.30–15.30, 19.30–23.00 Mon–Sat, closed Sun & two weeks Aug Ⓝ Funicular: Centrale to Augusteo; bus: C25

Ciro a Santa Brigida £ ⓫ While this eatery is technically a restaurant, it's best known for its pizza. ❸ Via Santa Brigida 71 ❶ (081) 552 4072 Ⓦ www.ciroasantabrigida.com ❶ 12.30–15.30, 19.30–24.00 Mon–Sat, closed Sun & two weeks Aug Ⓝ Funicular: Centrale to Augusteo; bus: C25, R2

La Locanda del Grifo £ ⓬ Traditional fare served in a convenient location. All the dishes are excellent and set off nicely by the selection of local wines. ❸ Via F del Giudice 14 ❶ (081) 442 0815 ❶ 12.00–15.30, 19.00–23.30 Mon & Wed–Sun, closed Tues Ⓝ Metro: Dante; bus: R1, R4

La Vecchia Cantina £ ⓭ A delightful *osteria* serving local specialities. As it's located next to the fish market, seafood dishes are good choices. ❸ Via San Nicola alla Carità 13–14 ❶ (081) 552 0226 ❶ 12.00–15.30, 20.00–23.00 Mon & Wed–Sat, 12.00–15.30 Tues & Sun, closed two weeks Aug Ⓝ Metro: Dante or Montesanto; bus: C57, R1, R4

Hosteria Toledo £–££ ⓮ Traditional dishes and local wine served in simple surroundings. ❸ Vico Giardinetto 78, off Via Toledo ❶ (081) 421 257 Ⓦ www.hosteriatoledo.it ❶ 12.00–15.00, 19.00–24.00 Mon & Wed–Sun, closed Tues Ⓝ Bus: C25, R2

Antica Osteria Pisano ££ ⓯ This tiny eatery is extremely popular and often packed. Traditional Neapolitan dishes are its speciality. ⓐ Piazzetta Crocelle ai Mannesi 1 ⓣ (081) 554 8325 ⓛ 12.00–16.00, 19.00–23.00 Mon–Sat, closed Sun & two weeks Aug ⓝ Metro: Dante or Museo; bus: R2

Bellini ££ ⓰ Enormous portions of seafood mixed with pasta. That's all they serve, and all you'll ever need. ⓐ Via Santa Maria di Constantinopoli 85 ⓣ (081) 459 774 ⓛ 12.30–15.30, 19.30–23.00 daily ⓝ Metro: Dante

La Cantina del Sole ££ ⓱ Most of the recipes used here date back to the 17th and 18th centuries. Dishes are extremely hearty and feature

△ Naples is filled to the gills with its own seafood specialities

intriguing flavours. ❷ Via Giovanni Paladino 37 ❶ (081) 552 7312
🕒 19.00–24.00 Mon–Sat, closed Sun ⓜ Metro: Dante; bus: R2

La Fila ££ ❿ A stone's throw from the central train station, the food
is exceptional. Try the buffet and let the chef suggest the rest.
❷ Via Nazionale 6/d ❶ (081) 206 717 🕒 13.00–15.00, 19.00–23.00
Tues–Sun, closed Mon ⓜ Metro: Garibaldi

BARS, CLUBS & DISCOS

Greenwich Pub A little bit of England in the heart of Naples. Mega
screens for football and a resident DJ. Heaven? ❷ Via San Giovanni
Maggiore Pignatelli 16 ❶ (081) 497 1246 🕒 19.00–03.00 daily
ⓜ Metro: Dante; bus: R1, R2

Rising South Comfy armchairs and sofas mix well with the
lounge music groove. ❷ Via San Sebastiano 19 ❶ (335) 879 0428
ⓦ www.risingsouth.it 🕒 22.00–03.00 Tues–Sun, closed Mon
& June–mid-Oct ⓜ Metro: Dante; bus: 24, E1, R1, R2

Superfly A jazz soundtrack provides the tunes. The whizz bar staff
provide the cocktails. You will, however, have to fight for one of the
six stools in this postage-stamp-sized bar. ❷ Via Cisterna dell'Olio 12
❶ (347) 127 2178 🕒 19.00–03.00 Tues–Sun, closed Mon & June–Sept
ⓜ Metro: Dante; bus: 24, R1, R2

Velvet Zone This dark and atmospheric nightclub is the best place to
dance the night away in the Centro Storico. ❷ Via Cisterna dell'Olio 11
❶ (339) 670 0234 ⓦ www.velvetnapoli.it 🕒 23.00–04.00 Wed, Thur &
Sun, 23.00–06.00 Fri & Sat, closed Mon, Tues & June–mid-Oct
ⓜ Metro: Dante; bus: 24, E1, R1, R2

CINEMAS & THEATRES

Bellini A theatre that stages everything from mainstream entertainment fare to local dance troupes. ⓐ Via Conte di Ruvo 14–19 ⓣ (081) 549 1266 ⓦ www.teatrobellini.it ⓛ Box office: 10.30–13.30, 16.00–19.00 Tues–Sat, 10.30–13.30, 16.00–17.30 Sun, closed Mon (Oct–May); performances: 21.00 Tues–Sat, 17.30 Wed & Sun ⓜ Metro: Piazza Cavour or Museo; bus: 24, R1, R2

Elicantropo This 40-seat theatre hosts fringe theatre and young companies looking to try out modern theatre pieces. ⓐ Vico Gerolomini 3 ⓣ (081) 296 640 ⓦ www.teatroelicantropo.com ⓛ Box office: 17.30–20.00 Oct–May; performances: 21.00 Oct–May ⓜ Metro: Piazza Cavour or Museo; bus: 149, CD, CS

Galleria Toledo A small, modern theatre hosting both cinema and new theatre projects. ⓐ Via Concezione a Montecalvario 34 ⓣ (081) 425 824 ⓦ www.galleriatoledo.org ⓛ Box office: 10.00–14.00, 15.00–18.00 Tues–Sun, closed Mon (Sept–May); performances: 20.30 Tues–Sun (Oct–May) ⓜ Metro: Montesanto; bus: E2

Modernissimo This complex of four cinemas is a local favourite, screening everything from Hollywood blockbusters to children's cartoons to arthouse classics. ⓐ Via Cisterna dell'Olio 23 ⓣ (081) 580 0254 ⓦ www.modernissimo.it ⓜ Metro: Dante; bus: 24, R1, R2

Teatro Nuovo The programme here is dedicated to the best new and international work. ⓐ Via Montecalvario 16 ⓣ (081) 406 062 or 406 062 ⓦ www.nuovoteatronuovo.it ⓛ Box office: 17.30–21.00 Tues & Wed, 11.00–12.30, 18.00–21.00 Thur–Sat, 16.30–18.00 Sun, closed Mon; performances: 21.00 Tues–Sat, 18.00 Sun (mid-Oct–May)

Vomero & Capodimonte

The two neighbourhoods of Capodimonte and Vomero are situated on the tops of hills. What distinguishes both areas from the city below is their relative peace and greenery. Capodimonte is sometimes seen as one massive park, with the museum (see page 91) situated in the centre. The grounds are a favourite spot for joggers, families and courting couples, especially at the weekend.

With its pedestrianised centre and cafés brimming with local residents, Via Scarlatti is the place to go in Vomero. While the Centro Storico is all about vibrant Neapolitan life, Vomero is much more middle class and subdued – a great change of pace if you can't take the constantly loud street theatre of the older parts of the city.

SIGHTS & ATTRACTIONS

Castel Sant'Elmo

The Castel Sant'Elmo can probably boast Naples' most glorious views. While not the original structure, the current building owes much of its look to additions made in the 16th century, when it gained its six-pointed star shape. A castle has existed at this strategic location overlooking the Bay of Naples since 1329, when Robert of Anjou constructed a fortification above a small church dedicated to St Erasmus (or Elmo).

A walk through the castle can be strangely spooky, especially during the gloomy winter months. Periodic temporary modern and experimental art collections do much to brighten up the surroundings, including displays in the dungeons on the first floor.

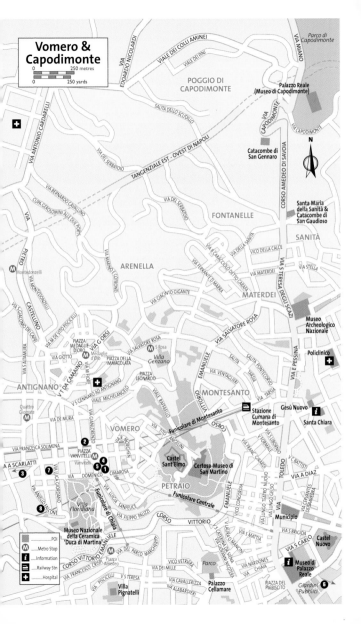

Vomero & Capodimonte

0   250 metres
0   250 yards

POGGIO DI CAPODIMONTE

Palazzo Reale (Museo di Capodimonte)

VIA MIANO

Parco di Capodimonte

VIALE DEI COLLI AMINEI

VIALE DEI PINI

VIA EDOARDO NICOLARDI

SALITA DELLO SCUDILLO

VIA CAPODIMONTE

Catacombe di San Gennaro

CORSO AMEDEO DI SAVOIA

VIA ANTONIO CARDARELLI

VIA DEL SERBATOIO

TANGENZIALE EST - OVEST DI NAPOLI

VIA BERNARDO CAVALLINO

CUPA GEROLOMINI ALLE DUE PORTE

VIA DEL SERBATOIO

FONTANELLE

Santa Maria della Sanità & Catacombe di San Gaudioso

SANITÀ

VIA PIETRO

VIA CASTELLINO

VIA MIANO E CORTONE

VIA 6 CARCCIOLO DETTO CARAFA

VIA DELLA SANITÀ

VICO DELLA CALCE

VIA MATERDEI

VIA STELLA

VIA TERESA DEGLI SCALZI

Montedonzelli Ⓜ

ARENELLA

VIA GIACINTO GIGANTE

VAL FERMENTO MARRA

MATERDEI

Museo Archeologico Nazionale

VIA GIACOMO DE CAPO

VIA C. ORSI

VIA SALVATORE ROSA

S. Rosa

VIA SALVATORE ROSA

VIA E FESSINA

VIA MON TEDONELLI

VIA SALTIMM

VIA M DE VITO PISCICELLI

PIAZZA MEDAGLIE D'ORO

Medaglie d'Oro Ⓜ

PIAZZA DELLA IMMACOLATA

Villa Genzano

SALITA PONTECORVO

SALITA TARSIA

VIA VENTAGLIERI

TARSIA

Policlinico ✚

VIA S ALTAMURA

VIA GIOTTO

VIA FIORE

VIA DA CAMANO

PIAZZA LEONARDO

VITTORIO EMANUELE

MONTESANTO

VIA SALTIMM

Gesù Nuovo ℹ

ANTIGNANO

VIA DE MURA

VIA S GENNARO AD ANTIGNANO

VIA MICHELANGELO

VIA RAFFAELLO

Funicolare di Montesanto

Stazione Cumana di Montesanto 🚉

Santa Chiara

Quattro Giornate Ⓜ

VIA FRANCESCA SOLIMENA

VOMERO

VIA TITO ANGELINI

VIA PESSINA

VIA S BIAGIO

VIA FRANC GIRALD

V C BATTISTI

A A SCARLATTI Ⓜ

PIAZZA VANVITELLI

❷

Vanvitelli Ⓜ

❹ ❺
❾ ❶

VIA CIMAROSA

Castel Sant'Elmo

Certosa-Museo di San Martino

VITTORIO EMANUELE

VICO LUNGO TEATRO NUOVO

VIA TOLEDO

VIA A DIAZ

❸

❼

VIA LUCA GIORDANO

VIA DOMENICO

PETRAIO

Funicolare Centrale

VIA CONCORDIA

VICO CONCORDIA

VIA LUNGO GELSO

VIA CERVANTES

❽

VIA ANIELLO FALCONE

Villa Floridiana

Funicolare di Chiaia

VIA LUCIA SANFELICE

VIA FILIPPO PALIZZI

CORSO

VITTORIO

VIA S MATTIA

VIA LAURA MANIN

Municipio

VIA S BRIGIDA

Museo Nazionale della Ceramica 'Duca di Martina'

CORSO VITTORIO EMANUELE

Piazza Amedeo Ⓜ

VIA DEL PARCO MARGHERITA

VIA CATERINA DA SIENA

VIA NARDONES

VIA CHIAIA

VIA S CARLO

Castel Nuovo

Museo di Palazzo Reale ℹ

VIA FRANCESCO CRISPI

V S TERESA

VICO VETRIERA

VIA PROCELLI

Parco

VIA DEI MILLE

VIA CAVALLERIZZA

Palazzo Cellamare

PIAZZA DEL PLEBISCITO

Giardini Pubblici ❻

Villa Pignatelli

VIA ALABARDIERI

■ POI
Ⓜ ......Metro Stop
ℹ ......Information
🚉 ......Railway Stn
✚ ......Hospital

ⓐ Via Tito Angelini 22 ☎ (081) 229 4401 🕐 08.30–19.30 Thur–Tues, closed Wed Ⓥ Funicular: Montesanto to Via Morghen, Centrale to Piazza Fuga or Chiaia to Via Cimarosa; bus: V1

Catacombe di San Gennaro

San Gennaro's charisma reaches down the years. Not only does he have a city in his thrall over two phials of his blood, he also gets to commune with the dead in a catacomb named after him. Two levels of catacombs contain some much-muddied frescoes dating back as far as the 2nd century AD. But it wasn't until the body of

🔵 *The Certosa-Museo di San Martino*

San Gennaro was brought here in the 5th century that the catacombs became a place of pilgrimage and worship. ❸ Via Capodimonte 13 ❶ (081) 741 1071 ❺ Guided tours only: 09.00, 10.00, 11.00, 12.00 Tues–Sun, closed Mon ❷ Bus: 24, 110, R2 ❶ Admission charge

CULTURE

Certosa-Museo di San Martino

The Museo di San Martino boasts one of the most intriguing collections of treasures in the city. To its credit, San Martino is more than just a museum. A former monastery, the grounds of the Certosa-Museo hold an art gallery, a collection of Nativity scenes and a church. The highlight of the collection is the fascinating Tavola Strozzi, a 3-D depiction of the city of Naples as it looked in the 15th century. ❸ Largo San Martino 5 ❶ (081) 578 1769 ❺ 08.30–19.30 Thur–Tues, closed Wed; last entry 18.30 ❷ Funicular: Montesanto to Via Morghen, Centrale to Piazza Fuga or Chiaia to Via Cimarosa; bus: V1 ❶ Admission charge

Museo di Capodimonte

Second only to the Museo Nazionale Archeologico (see page 78), this wonderful art museum holds the paintings of the celebrated Farnese Collection. A number of masterpieces, including works by Raphael and Titian, are showcased, including the latter's *Danae* (located in Room 11). Other big names exhibited include Botticelli, El Greco, Renoir, Caravaggio, Rembrandt and Tintoretto. ❸ Via Miano 2 ❶ (081) 749 9111 ❿ www.museo-capodimonte.it ❺ 08.30–19.30, Thur–Tues, closed Wed, reduced hours mid-Dec–mid-Jan ❷ Bus: 24, 110, R2 ❶ Admission charge

FUNICULAR FUN

Before the advent of the funicular railway in 1889, travellers to Vomero were forced to traverse a long flight of steps leading up from the city centre. Obviously, this prevented many visitors from making the journey.

Rides on the funicular railway proved to be so popular that a famous song was composed in the late 19th century, broadcasting its reputation. 'Funiculì, Funiculà' remains popular and can still be heard on many recordings – especially in the streets of the city that sparked the craze.

In total, four lines run between Vomero and the districts below. The longest funicular is the Centrale line, which begins its journey on Via Toledo and terminates near Via Scarlatti.

As only two trains run on each line at any given time (one going up, the other down), it can get extremely busy – especially during the traditional rush hours. If the trains are packed, walking up the steps remains an option, but only for the physically fit. On temperate days, it remains an enjoyable (if slightly tiring) journey.

Museo Nazionale della Ceramica 'Duca di Martina'

The world of ceramics is celebrated in this museum. The first floor is dedicated to the history of European work, including examples from Meissen and fine Capodimonte figurines. The ground level holds international pieces with a focus on Japanese and Chinese items. ❷ Via Cimarosa 77 ❶ (081) 578 8418 ❸ 08.30–14.00 Wed–Mon, closed Tues ❹ Funicular: Montesanto to Via Morghen,

Centrale to Piazza Fuga or Chiaia to Via Cimarosa; bus: E4, V1
❶ Admission charge

RETAIL THERAPY

As Vomero and Capodimonte are residential districts, you might think they would also have an abundance of shopping. But Naples follows centuries-old traditions: for a Neapolitan, shopping means a stroll through the Centro Storico (see page 74), the markets at La Pignasecca (see page 22) or the boutiques of Chiaia (see pages 65–8). Via Scarlatti in Vomero provides the best local options. A popular place for a wander, its pedestrianised centre is a great place to people-watch. Shops tend to focus more on household goods and basic needs in these quarters. Exceptions include bookshops and music shops catering to local intellectuals.

FNAC Branch of the French book chain. A limited number of books in English are stocked in case you need some holiday reading. Cinema and concert tickets are also available for purchase. ❸ Via Luca Giordano 59 ❶ (081) 220 1000 ❿ www.fnac.it ❶ 10.00–21.00 daily ❷ Funicular: Chiaia to Via Cimarosa, Centrale to Piazza Fuga; metro: Vanvitelli

Fonoteca Italy has plenty of bad Eurotrash music – but you won't find any of it in this eclectic music store. ❸ Via Morghen 31 C/D/E ❶ (081) 556 0338 ❶ 10.00–01.00 Mon–Wed, 10.00–02.00 Thur–Sat, 18.00–01.30 Sun ❷ Funicular: Chiaia to Via Cimarosa, Centrale to Piazza Fuga; metro: Vanvitelli; bus: C36

Studio K Designer furnishings, lamps and household items with modern flair. ❸ Via Cimarosa 81 ❶ (081) 556 5984 ❶ 10.00–13.30,

16.30–20.00 Mon–Sat, closed Sun & three weeks Aug Funicular: Chiaia to Via Cimarosa, Centrale to Piazza Fuga; bus: C36

TAKING A BREAK

Friggitoria Vomero £ ❶ On your way to the Castel Sant'Elmo but haven't had breakfast? Stop at this café for doughnuts and coffee. Via Domenico Cimarosa 44 ❶ (081) 578 3130 09.30–14.00, 17.00–21.30 Mon–Sat, closed Sun & Aug Funicular: Centrale to Piazza Fuga, Chiaia to Via Cimarosa; bus: C28, C31, C32, V1

La Polpetteria £ ❷ A recent addition to the food scene of Naples. This small restaurant offers 35 different types of *polpette* (meatballs), of which 15 are vegetarian options. Fun and reasonably priced. Via Francesco Solimena 79 ❶ (081) 1951 8381

Pizzeria Cilea £–££ ❸ Forget the diet just for a day and try the delicious *frittura*. One taste will have you return to the days when deep-fat fryers were all the rage. Via Cilea 43 ❶ (081) 556 3291 13.00–16.00, 19.30–23.00 Mon–Sat, 07.30–23.30 Sun, closed two weeks Aug Bus: 181, C31, C32

AFTER DARK

RESTAURANTS
Osteria Donna Teresa £ ❹ Don't even think about trying to leave in a rush, as the owner won't let you go until you finish every bite of two full courses. Don't worry, though, as the delicious traditional dishes will make you want to stay. Via Kerbaker 58 ❶ (081) 556 7070 12.30–15.00, 19.30–23.00 Mon–Sat, closed

● *A sunny spot and a slice of pizza*

Sun & Aug Funicular: Chiaia to Via Cimarosa, Centrale to Piazza Fuga; bus: C28, C31, C32

La Cantina di Sica £–££ ❺ Good for hearty traditional food, the Cantina di Sica excels with its pasta dishes. Some nights you'll find Neapolitan folk musicians playing in the wine bar. ❷ Via Bernini 17 ❶ (081) 556 7520 ⏰ 12.30–16.00, 20.00–24.00 Tues–Sun, closed Mon & one week Aug ❂ Funicular: Chiaia to Via Cimarosa, Centrale to Piazza Fuga; bus: C28, C31, C32, V1

Da Cicciotto ££ ❻ Once you find this restaurant, you will never want to leave. Blame it on the fantastic view, the secluded atmosphere or the unbeatable menu of fresh fish. Allow extra time to find it, or simply take a cab. ❷ Calata Ponticello a Marechiaro 32 ❶ (081) 575 1165 ⓦ www.trattoriadacicciotto.it ⏰ 12.30–15.00, 20.00–24.00 daily ❂ Bus: C31, C32, V1

Il Giardino del Pontano ££ ❼ Via Scarlatti is the heart of Vomero, essentially cutting the district in two. This cosy eatery, just off the pedestrianised main drag, is a real find for a casual evening. A little courtyard with a garden holds a few tables for alfresco dining. Occasional theme evenings based on the tastes of specific Italian regions are sometimes held. ❷ Via Luca Giordano 99 ❶ (081) 658 4699 ⏰ 13.00–15.00, 20.00–24.00 daily, closed two weeks Aug ❂ Funicular: Chiaia to Via Cimarosa, Centrale to Piazza Fuga; bus: C28, C31, C32, V1

D'Angelo Santa Caterina ££–£££ ❽ A dreamy eatery set amid stunning gardens with inspiring views of the city. For a romantic meal, this is the place to go. The seafood antipasti are

particularly tasty. ❸ Via Aniello Falcone 203 ❶ (081) 578 9772
Ⓦ www.ristorantedangelo.com ❺ 12.30–22.30 Mon & Wed–Sat,
13.00–15.30 Sun, closed Tues & two weeks Aug Ⓝ Bus: C28

BARS, CLUBS & DISCOS

Baik Set in the posh neighbourhood of Vomero, this is a great
place to people-watch. ❸ Via Aniello Falcone 372 ❶ (339) 746 7204
Ⓦ www.baikwinebar.it ❺ 19.00–04.00 daily, closed two weeks in
Aug Ⓝ Metro: Vanvitelli; bus: C28

⬥ *The occidental Miami Bar Room*

Bocca d'Oro Technically a restaurant, this popular Vomero rest-stop is a good place to start an evening, mainly because of its extensive wine list. ⓐ Piazzetta Durante 1 ⓣ (081) 229 2010 ⓛ 12.30–16.00, 20.30–02.00 Tues–Sat, 20.30–24.00 Mon & Sun, closed Aug ⓝ Funicular: Chiaia to Via Cimarosa, Centrale to Piazza Fuga; bus: C28, C31, C32

Miami Bar Room As close to Florida as you will be in Naples. Stark interior design, lounge music and a hip crowd make this a popular place. ⓐ Via Morghen 68/c ⓣ (081) 229 8332 ⓦ www.miamibarroom.it ⓛ 22.00–02.00 daily, closed Aug

CINEMAS & THEATRES
Plaza A cinema that shows English-language features on Tuesday evenings. ⓐ Via Kerbaker 85 ⓣ (081) 556 3555 ⓝ Metro: Vanvitelli

ⓞ *Mount Vesuvius looms over Naples*

OUT OF TOWN
trips

Herculaneum, Vesuvius & Pompeii

Many say that the purpose of a trip to Naples is not to visit the city itself, but to see everything that surrounds it. No attractions back up this claim more than the excavated remains of the towns of Herculaneum (Ercolano) and Pompeii, destroyed by a massive eruption of Vesuvius in 79 AD.

Today, these remains are the most visited attractions on the Campanian coastline – and justifiably so. The riches in these popular Roman getaway communities must have been immense, judging by the frescoes and artefacts that have been uncovered since the days when the Bourbons began digging up the area. While many of the most priceless treasures have been carted off to the Museo Nazionale Archeologico in Naples (see page 78), you can still get a strong sense of what Roman life must have been like simply by looking at the remaining structures.

Despite the constant eruptions, Herculaneum rebuilt itself and is now one of the most densely populated towns in Europe. Much of the Ercolano site remains uncovered due to the volume of humanity that lives above. Who knows what treasures lie beneath?

GETTING THERE

This area can be reached by road, but the journey can be both hair-raising and stress-inducing. It makes a lot more sense to take the train. The company **Circumvesuviana** (❶ (081) 772 2444 or toll-free within Italy on 800 053 939 ❿ www.vesuviana.it) has a service that connects Naples to all three sites. If you do decide to drive, use the A3 motorway.

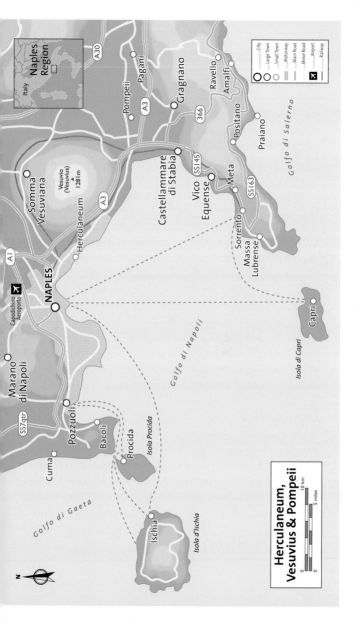

Herculaneum,
Vesuvius & Pompeii

SIGHTS & ATTRACTIONS

Herculaneum

It could be argued that the treasures of Herculaneum are even greater than the remains of Pompeii (see pages 106–10). What gives this site its secondary status is the fact that much of it exists buried under the existing city of concrete and precarious tower blocks.

Most residents were killed when a shift in the winds and heavy rainfall transformed the earth into a sea of mud, lava and ash that hurtled down on top of the city. When the devastation stopped, the ground level had risen by over 20 m (65 ft), obliterating the entire city from sight.

Archaeologists were both hindered and helped by this volume of mud. Digging through thick layers of earth under a heavily populated city is extremely challenging. Luckily, the mud also served to protect the ancient structures and all the buildings are in a better state of preservation than those at Pompeii.

SCAVI DI ERCOLANO – HERCULANEUM EXCAVATED

Legend has it that Herculaneum was founded by Hercules during his return from Iberia. Even though only a small section of the town has been excavated, what has been dug up reveals that Herculaneum was a centre of great importance to the Roman Empire. Luxurious residences stood on the promontory and the lack of any wheel ruts in the paving stones indicates that there wasn't much passing trade. As such, it is believed that the area was reserved for the mega-wealthy who chose to live here in order to enjoy the beauty and tranquillity of the region.

⬤ The street excavations at Herculaneum

● *Pompeii with its nemesis Mount Vesuvius in the background*

Mount Vesuvius

Naples – just like the rest of Campania – lives and dies by the moans and mutterings of Mount Vesuvius. One might think that the residents of one of Europe's most densely populated regions would be mad to choose to live next to an active volcano. The most recent volcanic eruption occurred in 1944. Evidence of the lava flow from that explosion is still visible close to the remains at Pompeii – and that's not taking into account the earthquakes that often occur in volcanic regions. Scientists often say that the 'big one' is right around the corner. So why do the locals stay? The main reason is agriculture. Campanian soil is extra rich in nutrients. Crops flourish remarkably well in the region and local produce is considered top-notch. That, combined with a gorgeous climate, incredible topography, beautiful islands and waters stocked with seafood, translate into a glorious lifestyle.

Cratere del Vesuvio

Vesuvius may look calm at a distance, but a hike up close reveals the truth. This deceptive peak has killed thousands and continues to worry the experts of the **Osservatorio Vesuviano** (☎ (081) 610 8300 Ⓦ www.ov.ingv.it), the institute that has been monitoring the volcano's activity ever since 1841.

A walk up the peak is a popular pastime and well worth considering even if you aren't a regular hiker. Declared a UNESCO Biosphere Reserve, the volcano is a protected plot of land attracting 200,000 visitors each year. Hiking is permitted right to the rim of the cone, allowing visitors the opportunity to peek into the depths of the crater 200 m (650 ft) below.

A hike up the mountain works best in May and early June when mornings tend to be calm and clear. Setting off on a windy day is not advised, as conditions can be challenging.

A standard 30-minute route takes visitors from the car park to the rim along a well-maintained path. The car park is located at the end of the road on the volcano's west side.

The most intriguing structure is a museum and observatory chronicling the volcano's history – but not for the displays. What most fascinates is the question of how the Bourbon-era building has managed to survive at least seven eruptions without a sign of damage!
🄐 Cratere del Vesuvio 🄣 (081) 771 0939 🄦 www.vesuviopark.it/grancono 🄛 09.00–two hours before sunset 🄘 Admission charge

Pompeii

Pompeii was immortalised on 24 August 79 AD when Vesuvius erupted in a sea of lava, ash and sulphurous gases. Residents initially thought they were out of firing range and many stayed to weather the storm. A rapidly moving, super-heated cloud of gases made them regret this decision, killing many as they huddled in their homes. The cloud occurred so suddenly that, when archaeologists dug up Pompeii centuries later, they were able to make plaster casts from the spaces formed by bodies that had long since disintegrated. Several were performing everyday tasks, causing many to believe that the cloud must have overcome people almost instantly.

By the time of the eruption, Pompeii was a city in decline. While it was still a favoured playground for the rich of the Roman Empire, its status was far from the glory days of a mere two centuries earlier, when its importance rivalled even that of Naples.

Pompeii owed its popularity to its strategic position near the River Sarno. Buildings were developed using Greek techniques, resulting in a well-ordered grid pattern. Roads were paved from slabs of old lava, while the villas and houses of the rich and powerful were constructed from stone, brick and cement – many highly decorated.

Streets, workshops and public areas are in a wonderful state of preservation, and there is much more to uncover. Recent roadworks on the Naples–Salerno motorway revealed a frescoed leisure complex. Treasures such as jewellery, tools, furnishings and even

⬤ *One of Pompeii's many victims*

PROFITS OF DOOM

Residents of Campania are familiar with natural disasters, but they also know how to turn a profit once the dust has cleared. Locals are still coping with the effects of the 1980 earthquake, which killed thousands. On top of that, mass corruption sucked millions from the coffers of the regional government as unscrupulous developers built shoddy, unregulated tower blocks up and down the coast.

This phenomenon is not new. Emperor Vespasian noticed the same problems when he sent a tribune to enforce zoning laws following the earthquake of 62 AD.

preserved food and drink have provided key insights into how the Romans lived, both as slaves and as citizens.

CULTURE

Scavi di Pompeii

The ruins at Pompeii are among the most visited sights in all of Italy and have been almost since the day they were uncovered in 1750. Historians of the day unearthed the site using techniques that would make modern-day archaeologists shudder in horror. Along with the bodies of the dead, treasures including magnificent frescoes, temples and everyday objects were dug up and shipped to the Museo Nazionale Archeologico (see page 78).

Today, the ruins look a little the worse for wear: the sheer volume of visitors is having its effect. The most important structures to view are the great houses concentrated along Via dell'Abbondanza and between Via del Mercurio in the northwest of Pompeii and Via Stabiana. The homes of the wealthiest residents are easily spotted as they feature courtyards, living rooms and – the most prized possession of all – private gardens. A typical home is focused

⬥ *Fresco from a house in Pompeii*

around two open courts, each featuring elements of Greek and Italian architecture.

Lupanare, the main brothel of the city of Pompeii, is definitely worth a visit for the great frescoes that give us an idea of daily life in the city.

When visiting Pompeii, it is best to bring plenty of water and a hat. There is very little shade available anywhere on-site and crowds can get claustrophobic. To avoid the bulk of the visitors, go later in the day when tour buses are long gone. ⓐ Porta Marina ⓣ (081) 857 5347 ⓦ www.pompeiisites.org ⓛ 08.30–19.30 daily, ticket office closes 18.00 (Apr–Oct); 08.30–17.00, ticket office closes 15.30 (Nov–Mar) ⓘ Admission charge

Suggestioni al Foro
Touring the ruins of Pompeii after dark is a possibility thanks to a tour that takes a limited number of travellers through the civic and religious buildings that surround the main square. While the number of rooms on view is small, seeing everything accompanied by a few torches and some 'arty' lighting enhances the experience of seeing the ruins – especially as you aren't surrounded by hundreds of package tourists. ⓣ (347) 346 0346 ⓛ Tours in English vary, call ahead ⓘ Reservations obligatory

AFTER DARK

Il Principe £££ This restaurant is one of Campania's finest. Dishes are all drawn from history, including recipes from ancient authors. ⓐ Piazza B Longo 1, Pompeii ⓣ (081) 850 5566 ⓦ www.ilprincipe.com ⓛ 12.30–15.30, 19.00–23.30 Tues–Sat, 12.30–15.30 Sun & Mon (Apr–Oct); 12.30–15.30, 19.00–23.30 Tues–Sat, 12.30–15.30 Sun, closed

Mon (Nov–Mar); closed three weeks Aug ⓝ Circumvesuviana to Pompeii Scavi – Villa dei Misteri

ACCOMMODATION

Casa del Pellegrino £ A well-placed hostel offering both dorms and private family rooms in a converted convent. Furnishings are basic. ⓐ Via Duca D'Aosta 4 ⓣ (081) 850 8644 ⓝ Train: Circumvesuviana to Pompeii Scavi – Villa dei Misteri

Hotel Amleto £–££ This quaint property is located steps away from the entrance to the archaeological zone. Rooms are themed in a variety of 'old' Italian styles, some featuring attractive *trompe l'œil* wall paintings. ⓐ Via B Longo 10 ⓣ (081) 863 1004 ⓦ www.hotelamleto.it ⓝ Train: Circumvesuviana to Pompeii Scavi – Villa dei Misteri

🔺 *Sample some star-quality seafood*

The Amalfi Coast

The Amalfi Coast is one of nature's wonders. Rocky cliffs plunge into the Mediterranean, dotted with pastel-hued towns that cling precariously to the peninsula. The visuals would inspire anyone – and often have. Authors as diverse as Steinbeck, Shelley, Byron and Goethe have explored the region and marvelled over its beauty. That said, living here hasn't always been so delightful. Until roads were carved out of the cliffs, residents were cut off from the rest of Italy and subject to constant pirate raids and storms.

Today, the attacks come in the form of crowds of tourists and massive tour buses that clog the roads every summer weekend. If you are planning a drive along the coast – and it is surely one of the world's most beautiful driving itineraries – avoid a trip during the weekend when the coast road turns into a car park.

The traditional drive begins in Sorrento and follows the 145 until Amalfi. Some intrepid travellers continue the journey to Ravello if they have the time. If you are a nervous driver, consider booking yourself on a tour. While you won't have the same flexibility, the road has enough hairpin turns to make even Lewis Hamilton fearful. Be very careful when passing as the road is barely big enough for one car, let alone two. Above all, the key to enjoyment is stopping. Don't get sucked into the monotony of the drive, for it is the exploration of the individual towns along the way that will provide the most memorable moments.

GETTING THERE

Roads to Sorrento and the Amalfi Coast are narrow and always crowded, so unless you have hired a driver your best bet is to rely on

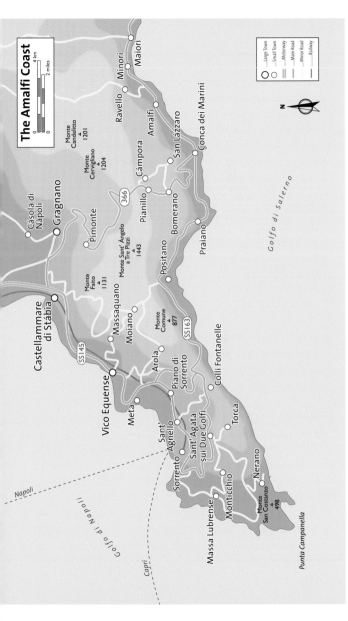

public transport. The Circumvesuviana line (see page 100) runs every
40 minutes from Naples Piazza Garibaldi station. Buses leave twice
a day from the airport. In the tourist seasons, you can also take the
Metro del Mare from Molo Beverello (ⓦ www.metrodelmare.net).
As with all destinations on the Amalfi Coast, Positano is better
reached by public transportation. Buses leave every morning from
Piazza del Municipio (ⓦ www.sitabus.it).

AMALFI

The Amalfi Coast gets its name from this beautiful town, which
seems to cling to the rock face it sits on. Once a powerful maritime
republic, the area boomed during the 11th century when it was one
of Italy's richest cities – rivalling Venice and Genoa in trade volume
and traffic.

Amalfi sailors were – and still are – respected. For many years,
the bulk of residents made their fortunes hiring themselves out
as marine mercenaries terrorising the high seas. Little evidence
remains of the days when Amalfi boasted a population of 60,000.
What is left, however, is a joy to wander through and savour.

SIGHTS & ATTRACTIONS
Duomo di Amalfi
Amalfi's main church was founded in the 9th century and has been
rebuilt many times. The structure is a combination of styles
ranging from Italian Romanesque to neoclassical. Surprisingly, the
mish-mash works. The only part of the church that has survived
since its original construction is the Cappella del Crocefisso, which
holds the major treasures of the church, including a 15th-century
bas-relief and a bejewelled mitre. ⓐ Piazza del Duomo

🔺 *Take time out on the beach at Amalfi*

☏ (089) 871 1324 **🕐** 09.00–19.00 (Apr–June); 09.00–21.00 (July–Sept); 09.30–17.00 (Oct & Mar); 10.00–13.00, 14.30–16.30 (Nov–Feb) **❶** Admission charge

⬢ *Amalfi's cathedral is a wonderful mish-mash of styles*

CULTURE
Museo della Carta

The valley that surrounds Amalfi was known for centuries as the site of some of Europe's leading paper manufacturers. One of the original factories has now been transformed into a museum illustrating the history and techniques of the trade. ⓐ Via delle Cartiere 24 ⓣ (089) 830 4561 ⓦ www.museodellacarta.it ⓛ 10.00–18.30 daily (Mar–Oct); 10.00–15.30 Tues–Sun, closed Mon (Nov–Feb)

RETAIL THERAPY

Antichi Sapori d'Amalfi Delightful selection of home-made *limoncello* and fruit liqueurs. ⓐ Piazza del Duomo 39 ⓣ (089) 872 062 ⓦ www.antichisaporidamalfi.it ⓛ 11.00–15.30, 16.00–19.30 Mon–Wed, Fri & Sat, 09.30–13.30, 15.30–20.00 Sun, closed Thur

La Scuderia del Duca Purchase some beautiful handmade paper or choose from a selection of books on Amalfi from this delightfully old-fashioned stationery shop. ⓐ Largo Cesareo Console 8 ⓣ (089) 872 976 ⓦ www.carta-amalfi.it ⓛ 11.00–15.30, 16.30–19.00 Tues–Sat, closed Sun, Mon & Jan

AFTER DARK
Restaurants

Da Maria £–££ Your head will spin at the sheer number of cheap pizzerias and trattorias that have set up business in Amalfi. Da Maria features the same menu and prices as the rest, but the food is somehow a touch better than the average rest-stop. The seafood pastas and pizzas are especially good. ⓐ Via Lorenzo d'Amalfi 14 ⓣ (089) 873 451 ⓛ 12.00–15.00, 19.30–22.30 Tues–Sun, closed Mon & Nov

La Caravella £££ The fact that this restaurant is always full should give you a good clue that it is considered Amalfi's best restaurant. Seafood is a highlight. ⓐ Via Matteo Camera 12 ⓣ (089) 871 029 ⓦ www.ristorantelacaravella.it ⓛ 12.00–14.30, 19.30–22.30 Mon, Wed–Sun, closed Tues & mid-Nov–Dec

Bars & clubs
Bar Risacca A favoured place for breakfast by day or a Campari and soda by night. ⓐ Piazza Umberto I 16 ⓣ (089) 872 866 ⓦ www.risacca.com ⓛ 09.00–15.00, 19.00–24.00 daily (Apr–Oct); 09.00–15.00, 19.00–24.00 Tues–Sun, closed Mon (Nov–Mar)

RoccoCò The usual pop anthems played by different DJs throughout the year. Good if you're in need of letting down your hair and dancing the night away. ⓐ Via delle Cartiere 98 ⓣ (089) 873 080 ⓛ 22.00–03.00 daily (Apr–Oct); 22.00–03.00 Fri & Sat, closed Sun–Thur (Nov–Mar)

ACCOMMODATION
Amalfi £–££ This quality 3-star is the town's best moderate option. Service is efficient, but the property can sometimes feel like it's been overrun by British tour groups. ⓐ Vico dei Pastai 3 ⓣ (089) 872 440 ⓦ www.hamalfi.it

Santa Caterina £££ A stunning 5-star property located just west of Amalfi towards Positano. The hotel has a stretch of private beach all to itself – but you may not even step on it as you can enjoy the sun's rays from the comfort of your private terrace. ⓐ SS Amalfitana 9 ⓣ (089) 871 012 ⓦ www.hotelsantacaterina.it

POSITANO

Probably the Amalfi Coast's most visually stunning town, Positano is a precariously perched community that found its place on the tourist map in the 1950s following years of decline. During the 18th and 19th centuries, many locals emigrated, unable to continue facing the harsh conditions, pirate attacks and being detached from the rest of the country. When roads finally opened the region up to the outside world, the outside world moved in to take advantage of the glorious lifestyle this cliff community had to offer.

RETAIL THERAPY

La Libreria Itaka This bookshop fits the bill if you need some holiday reading material. The English-language selection is limited, but there is a nice range of local guidebooks if you need further inspiration. ● Via Colombo 165 ● (089) 811 077 ● 11.30–15.00, 16.00–19.00 Tues–Sat, closed Sun, Mon & mid-Nov–Feb

AFTER DARK

Restaurants

Donna Rosa ££ This elegant trattoria boasting views over the main village is an extremely romantic spot for a meal. ● Via Montepertuso 69 ● (089) 811 806 ● 19.00–23.30 (Aug); 19.00–23.00 Mon & Tues, 12.00–16.00, 19.00–23.00 Wed–Sun (May–July, Sept, Oct); 12.00–16.00, 19.00–23.00 Mon, Wed–Sun (Apr, Nov, Dec); closed Jan–Mar

Il Capitano £££ Locals and holidaymakers agree that Il Capitano is Positano's best restaurant. Dishes are classic and delicious. Fish dishes are especially recommended. The views of the coast from the terrace

⬥ *The stunning seaside town of Positano*

are superb. ⓐ Via Pasitea 119 ❶ (089) 811 351 ⓦ www.hotelmontemare.it
🕒 12.30–15.00, 19.00–23.00 daily; closed Nov–Apr

Clubs & bars

Africana Hidden in a rocky cove, this amazing dance club features
a dance floor inside a grotto. Young people from across the Sorrentine
Peninsula make a beeline for this hotspot, especially in summer when
direct boats run to and from Salerno, Maiori, Minori and Amalfi. ⓐ West
of Marina di Praia, between Positano and Amalfi ❶ (089) 874 042
🕒 22.30–04.00 Wed–Sun; closed Mon & Tues (Oct–May)

ACCOMMODATION

La Rosa dei Venti ££ Reasonable prices and great views. The ambience might be Spartan but the quality is superior to the price.
ⓐ Via Fornillo 40 ⓣ (089) 875 252 ⓦ www.larosadeiventi.net

San Pietro £££ The San Pietro could well be the most exclusive hotel in Italy. Constructed from a private villa just 1 km (½ mile) east of Positano, a tiny sign by the side of the road is the only indication of its existence. Rooms feature jacuzzis and private balconies, and a lift takes guests down to the beach. Worth the (major) splurge.
ⓐ Via Laurito 2 ⓣ (089) 875 455 ⓦ www.ilsanpietro.it

SORRENTO

A favourite with British tourists ever since the days of the 'grand tour', Sorrento is the gateway to the Sorrentine Peninsula and a popular starting point for the famed drive along the Amalfi Coast. It may seem that package tourists have overrun the place, but it's easy to escape the English pubs and blue-rinse brigade to discover the magic that brought all these people here in the first place.

SIGHTS & ATTRACTIONS
Duomo
The original cathedral of Sorrento was rebuilt in the Gothic style. Fine examples of local *intarsio* (wooden inlay) work decorate the choir stalls. Of particular note is the bishop's throne dating from 1573, constructed from marble fragments. ❷ Corso Italia ❶ (081) 878 2248 ❸ 07.40–12.00, 16.30–20.30 daily

CULTURE
Museo Correale di Terranova
Here you'll find a jumbled collection of local art and artefacts left to the town by two brothers in the 1920s. The archaeological section boasts the best exhibits, including a collection of Greek and Roman marbles, Greek classical sculptures and vases. There are also minor works of the 17th and 18th centuries from the Neapolitan school of painters and artists. ❷ Via Correale 48 ❶ (081) 878 1846 ❸ 09.00–14.00 Wed–Mon, closed Tues ❶ Admission charge

Museobottega della Tarsialignea
This museum, situated in a restored 18th-century *palazzo*, displays the best of local handicraft and artwork including stunning

◆ *Impressive cliff-top mansions in Sorrento*

examples of wooden inlay furniture. Old paintings and photographs of Sorrento provide additional context. ⓐ Via San Nicolo 28 ⓣ (081) 877 1942 ⓦ www.alessandrofiorentinocollection.it ⓛ 09.30–13.00, 16.00–20.00 Tues–Sun (Apr–Oct); 09.30–13.00, 15.00–19.00 Tues–Sun (Nov–Mar); closed Mon

RETAIL THERAPY

Pepe Traditional ceramics and more modern pieces, great for gifts and keepsakes. ⓐ Piazza S Antonino 17 ⓣ (081) 877 3984 ⓛ 10.00–19.00 Mon–Sat, closed Sun

Salvatore Gargiulo Sorrento's best furniture workshop specialising in marquetry and wooden inlay. ⓐ Via Fuoro 33 ⓣ (081) 878 2420 ⓦ www.gargiuloinlaid.it ⓛ 09.30–13.00, 16.00–19.00 Tues–Sun, closed Mon

TAKING A BREAK

Bar Ercolano £ Lovely outdoor café that's perfect for people-watching. Service is slow, but the quality of the ice cream compensates. ⓐ Piazza Tasso ⓣ (081) 807 2951 ⓛ 06.00–01.30 Mon & Wed–Sun (Apr–Sept); 06.00–22.30 Mon & Wed–Sun (Oct–Mar); closed Tues

Il Fauno ££ Of all the cafés in the centre, this is the most chic. The high end of society wouldn't be caught anywhere else. People-watching possibilities are superb and the range of beverages is delicious. ⓐ Piazza Tasso 13–15 ⓣ (081) 878 1135 ⓦ www.faunobar.it ⓛ 07.00–24.00 daily

AFTER DARK
Restaurants
Da Emilia £ Unassuming family-run restaurant with friendly service and traditional, hearty cuisine. Grab a chair at one of the

wooden tables and enjoy. ⓐ Marina Grande 62 ⓣ (081) 807 2720
ⓛ 12.30–15.00, 19.30–23.30 daily (July & Aug); 12.30–15.00,
19.00–23.30 Mon & Wed–Sun, closed Tues (Apr–June, Sept & Oct);
call in advance to check Nov–Mar

Ristorante Vittoria ££ Step back in time and imagine you're on a
'grand tour' through Italy in the 19th century. White-jacketed waiters
put on a formal display of 'old-school' service. Dishes are hit and
miss, but it's the atmosphere and the frescoed dining room that
continue to draw in the crowds. ⓐ Grand Hotel Excelsior Vittoria,
Piazza Tasso 34 ⓣ (081) 877 7111 ⓛ 12.30–14.00, 19.30–22.30 daily

Cinemas & theatres
Estate Musicale Sorrentina Sorrento's summer season of live
performances. Most concerts are free of charge and good quality.
Check listings on the website. ⓦ www.estatemusicalesorrentina.it

ACCOMMODATION
Ostello delle Sirene (Youth Hostel) £ If your budget can't quite
afford 5-star luxury but you still want to stay in Sorrento, check
into the youth hostel. The accommodation is basic, but the hostel
provides the cheapest beds in town. ⓐ Via degli Aranci 160 ⓣ (081)
807 2925 ⓦ www.hostellesirene.com

Imperial Hotel Tramontano £££ There are many 5-star properties
in Sorrento, but this is the pick for a truly special holiday. Shelley,
Byron, Goethe and Ibsen all enjoyed this hotel. Its cliff-side
location, beautiful pool and private beach will no doubt bring
you great pleasure too. ⓐ Via Veneto 1 ⓣ (081) 878 2588
ⓦ www.hoteltramontano.it

Capri, Ischia & Procida

The islands of Capri, Ischia and Procida are stunning. Sleepy during the winter months – you probably won't find anyone here in January or February except for a few die-hard natives and a couple of cats – the islands positively boom the minute the sun starts to heat their pebbly beaches.

Each island has its own characteristics and fans. Capri, with its designer boutiques and range of extortionate hotels, appeals to new money and youthful exuberance. Ischia is more for the established old-money set and those looking for quiet, calm and relaxation. Finally, there's Procida – a jewel of an island made for sleepy days in the sun and quiet meals under the stars.

GETTING THERE

By water

Reaching the islands during the summer couldn't be easier. Ferries and hydrofoils leave regularly from the Molo Beverello in Naples. There are also frequent services from Mergellina, Pozzuoli, Sorrento and Positano.

CAPRI

The brashest of Campania's holiday islands, Capri has been a favourite of artists for centuries. Everyone from the Roman Emperor Tiberius to W H Auden has been entranced by the island's topography, especially its famed Blue Grotto (see page 128). Tiberius was so bewitched by Capri that he temporarily moved the capital of the Roman Empire to its shores.

Heading out to the Blue Grotto

Today, Capri is best known as a millionaire's playground, complete with high-end designer boutiques, swish cafés serving €5 cups of coffee and exclusive resorts.

Due to space limitations, recommendations in this section will be limited to the offerings close to Capri Town. For more detailed descriptions of Anacapri and the rest of the island, please refer to *Travellers Naples & Amalfi Coast* – another title in the Thomas Cook Publishing range of guidebooks.

SIGHTS & ATTRACTIONS
Grotta Azzurra (Blue Grotto)
If there is one sight to see on Capri, then this is it. The mysterious blue hue is created by the refraction of light. The colour has inspired more than a few artists, especially during the 19th century, when poets raved about its mystical qualities. ● 09.00–one hour before sunset

Museo Villa San Michele
This small museum is in a beautiful villa, surrounded by an Italian garden. The villa hosts a collection of marbles and mosaics from the Etruscan and medieval periods. ● Viale Axel Munthe 34 ● (081) 837 1401 ● www.sanmichele.org ● 09.00–18.00 (May–Sept), 09.00–17.00 (Oct & Apr), 09.00–15.30 (Nov–Feb), 09.00–16.30 Mar ● Admission charge

RETAIL THERAPY
Limoncello di Capri This boutique created the famous lemon liqueur now available all across Campania. This is the place to buy a bottle. Drink it straight or on ice – but always chilled. ● Via Roma 79 ● (081) 837 3059 ● www.limoncello.com ● 11.00–19.30 daily (Apr–Oct); 11.00–14.30, 17.00–19.30 Tues–Sun, closed Mon (Nov–Mar)

TAKING A BREAK

Piccolo Bar There are four major bars on the Piazzetta – and there are very few differences between them. This establishment is the oldest on the square and offers great people-watching perches. ⓐ Piazzetta di Capri ⓣ (081) 837 0325 ⓛ 09.00–23.00 daily (Apr–Oct); 09.00–23.00 Tues–Sun, closed Mon (Nov–Mar)

AFTER DARK

Restaurants

La Capannina £££ This romantic, family-run establishment continues to draw the high and mighty of Capri. Come here for good old-fashioned cooking; this place has been serving its classic versions of traditional cuisine since it opened back in the 1930s. ⓐ Via Le Botteghe 12 bis ⓣ (081) 837 0732 ⓦ www.capannina-capri.com ⓛ 12.00–14.00, 19.30–24.00 daily (May–Sept); 12.00–14.00, 19.30–24.00 Mon, Tues & Thur–Sun, closed Wed (mid-Mar, Apr, Oct & 1st week Nov); closed 2nd week Nov–mid-Mar

Villa Verde £££ Where the stars come out to eat. Traditional Caprese food is this restaurant's speciality – and, boy, does it do it well. Despite the simple furnishings, this place is one of the most expensive on Capri. ⓐ Vico Sella Orta 6 ⓣ (081) 837 7024 ⓦ www.villaverde-capri.com ⓛ 12.00–15.30, 19.30–24.00 daily (Apr–Oct); 12.00–15.30, 19.30–24.00 Tues–Sun, closed Mon (Nov–Mar)

Cinemas & theatres

Arena The main cinema for Capri Town. Screenings are usually dubbed and have a leaning towards Hollywood blockbusters. ⓐ Vico Sella Orta 3 ⓣ (081) 837 4560

⬥ *The exquisite island of Capri*

ACCOMMODATION

Villa Eva £–££ Family-run, hidden on top of the island in the less crowded Anacapri. Here you will feel like you are in an oasis away from the crowds and the chaos. If you do not feel like heading to the beach, you can use the hotel pool, conveniently located in the centre of the property. ❸ Via La Fabbrica 8, Anacapri ❶ (081) 837 1549 ⓦ www.villaeva.com ❻ Closed Nov–Feb

Villa Sarah ££ Want to stay on Capri but don't have a Swiss bank account? This cheery Mediterranean villa should fit the bill. Expensive for what you get, it's still a bargain when compared to every other hotel in Capri Town. ❸ Via Tiberio 3A ❶ (081) 837 7817 ⓦ www.villasarah.it

Grand Hotel Quisisana £££ A Capri institution. Stay here if you want to mix with celebs and live the high life. ❸ Via Camerelle 2 ❶ (081) 837 0788 ⓦ www.quisisana.com ❻ Closed Nov–mid-Mar

J.K. Place £££ Brand new boutique hotel. Impeccable design, personable service and an unbeatable position. ❸ Prov Marina Grande 225 ❶ (081) 838 4001 ⓦ www.jkcapri.com ❻ Closed Nov–mid-Mar

ISCHIA

Many people have described Ischia as Capri's less-popular sister. While both are chic and boast amazing panoramas, Ischia is just that little less brash. Capri fans may have all the designer boutiques, but lovers of Ischia don't care. What they lack in designer duds they make up for in the form of natural spas, wider beaches and verdant hills.

The largest of all the islands off the Campanian coastline, Ischia can actually be divided into many regions. Due to space limitations, recommendations in this section will be limited to the offerings close to Ischia Porto. For more detailed descriptions of the island and its sights, please refer to *Travellers Naples & Amalfi Coast* – another title in the Thomas Cook Publishing range of guidebooks.

SIGHTS & ATTRACTIONS

Castello Aragonese

Originally fortified by the Greeks in the 5th century BC, this rocky outcrop has been used as a stronghold by Romans, Goths, Arabs and the British. The Castello found fame in the 16th century when it became home to the court of Vittoria Colonna, the wife of Ischia's feudal lord, Ferrante d'Avalos. Attacks during the 18th century forced 2,000 families to move behind its protected walls – and it took over a century before they decided to move back out. During this period, 13 churches were built on its grounds. Of all the attacking forces, it was the British who caused the most damage to the structure. During their bombardment of 1809, they aggressively attempted to remove the French from the island. Evidence of the battles can still be seen in the walls pockmarked by gunshot and shrapnel.
🕿 (081) 992 834 🔵 www.castelloaragonese.it 🕓 09.00–one hour before sunset (Mar–Nov); closed Dec–Feb

La Mortella

Lush, green gardens that house more than 3,000 rare varieties of plant life. The garden hosts concerts during the spring and summer.
🅐 Via F Calise 39, Forio 🕿 (081) 986 220 🔵 www.lamortella.org
🕓 09.00–19.00 Tues, Thur, Sat & Sun, closed Mon, Wed & Fri (Apr–end-Oct); closed end-Oct–end-Mar

Negombo

Created in 1946 by Duke Silvestro Camerini, the Negombo park is a beautiful oasis where plants, flowers and water merge to create a unique corner of the island. ❸ Baia di San Montano, Lacco Ameno ❶ (081) 986 152 Ⓦ www.negombo.it Ⓛ 08.30–19.00 daily

Terme di Cava Scura Spa

Ischia's most naturally beautiful spa, the Terme di Cava Scura is hewn out of rugged cliffs located at the end of one of Ischia's most stunning walking trails. Designed for the truly knowledgeable spa-goer, treatments include massages, facials and thermal baths in divine locations, including a natural cave. ❸ Via Cava Scura, Sant'Angelo d'Ischia ❶ (081) 905 564 Ⓦ www.cavascura.it Ⓛ 08.30–18.00 daily (mid-Apr–mid-Oct); closed end Oct–mid-Apr

⬢ Sant'Angelo – just one of Ischia's many pretty coastal villages

TAKING A BREAK

Da Ciccio £ The best ice cream on Ischia. No question. It's almost worth visiting the island just for a scoop if you can decide on just one flavour. ⓐ Piazza Antica Reggia 5 ⓣ (081) 991 314 ⓛ 07.00–24.00 daily (may close Mon in Nov & Jan)

Pane & Vino £ This late-closing shop sells exactly what you think – bread and wine. A great place to stock up for picnic supplies or prior to a ferry journey. ⓐ Via Porto 24 ⓣ (081) 991 046 ⓛ 10.00–02.00 daily (Apr–Oct); 10.00–13.00, 18.30–23.30 Mon, Tues & Thur–Sun, closed Wed (Nov–mid-Jan, Mar); closed mid-Jan–Feb

AFTER DARK
Restaurants

Cocò ££ Simple seafood and pasta dishes. The place is often filled with locals. ⓐ Piazzale Aragonese ⓣ (081) 981 823 ⓛ 12.30–15.00, 19.30–23.00 Mon, Tues & Thur–Sun, closed Wed (Mar, Apr, Oct–Dec); 12.30–15.00, 19.30–23.00 daily (May–Sept); closed Jan & Feb

Alberto a Mare £££ Shell out happily for the dishes at this lovely restaurant that sits on a platform overlooking the sea. It's hard to know which is more inspiring, the sunset or the food. ⓐ Passeggiata Cristoforo Colombo 8 ⓣ (081) 981 259 ⓛ 12.00–15.00, 19.00–23.00 daily; closed Nov–mid-Mar

Bars, clubs & discos

Bar Calice The streets around this buzzy bar may turn you off – but if you decide not to go, you'll be missing out on some of the island's best ice cream and cakes. A great place for a late-night coffee and chat. ⓐ Piazza degli Eroi 69 ⓣ (081) 991 270 ⓛ 07.00–02.00 daily (Apr–Oct); 07.00–02.00 Mon, Tues & Thur–Sun, closed Wed (Nov–Mar)

Oh! X Bacco This jolly wine bar serves tasty nibbles. If you're in a large group, consider ordering the *menu degustazione*, which provides a variety of antipasti samples. ⓐ Via Luigi Mazzella 20 ① (081) 991 354 ⓛ 11.00–15.00, 19.00–02.00 Mon & Wed–Sun (Mar–Oct); 18.00–24.00 Mon & Wed, 11.00–15.00, 18.00–24.00 Thur–Sun (Nov–Feb); closed Tues

ACCOMMODATION

Miramare e Castello ££–£££ Located directly on the beach, this is a lovely hotel for a relaxing break. Choose from rooms with or without a terrace depending on your budget. Spa packages are available. ⓐ Via Pontano 9 ① (081) 991 333 ⓦ www.miramareecastello.it ⓛ Closed mid-Oct–mid-Apr

Il Moresco £££ White Moorish arches and wrought-iron gratings combine to create this sublime hotel. Lose yourself in the gardens or take a dip in the thermal pool located in a rocky cave. ⓐ Via E Gianturco 16 ① (081) 981 355 ⓦ www.ilmoresco.it ⓛ Closed mid-Oct–mid-Apr

PROCIDA

The main port of Procida has been in existence almost since the days the Greeks first explored the region in the 5th century BC. Today, the architecture is highly influenced by the mini population boom of the 17th and 18th centuries when neoclassical looks were all the rage.

SIGHTS & ATTRACTIONS
Abbazia di San Michele Arcangelo
Dating back to 1026, the abbey has been rebuilt a number of times. The building has a painting of the archangel Michael by Luca

Giordano, a large manuscript museum, a Nativity scene and labyrinthine catacombs that lead to a secret chapel. ⓐ Via Canalone 1 ① (081) 896 7612 ① 10.00–12.45, 15.00–18.00 Mon–Sat, 09.45–12.45 Sun

Castello d'Avalos

You may not be able to enter the foreboding walls today, but up until 1986, you wouldn't have wanted to. Castello d'Avalos was Italy's answer to Alcatraz – an island prison where only the worst offenders were sent. The massive structure is the first building you see when arriving at Procida's Marina Grande. As yet, there are no plans to open up the building as a tourist attraction.

TAKING A BREAK

Bar del Cavaliere The local bourgeoisie love sipping cocktails at this lively bar on Via Roma. ⓐ Via Roma 42 ① (081) 810 1074 ① 12.30–15.30, 19.00–23.00 daily (Apr–Sept); 12.30–15.30, 19.00–23.00 Tues–Sun, closed Mon (Oct–Mar)

Bar Roma Delicious cakes are on offer at this casual bar next to the church of Santa Maria della Pietà. Order a coffee and cake and forget about the diet. ⓐ Via Roma 164 ① (081) 896 7460 ① 12.00–15.00, 19.00–23.00 (May–Sept); 12.00–15.00, 19.00–23.00 Mon & Wed–Sun, closed Tues (Oct–Apr)

AFTER DARK
Restaurants

Fammivento £–££ If you want to enjoy the hustle and bustle of the Marina Grande, choose this restaurant for its service with a smile. ⓐ Via Roma 39 ① (081) 896 9020 ① 12.30–15.30, 19.00–23.00 Tues–Sun,

⬥ *Wander through the narrow streets of Procida*

closed Mon (Mar–June & Sept–Dec); 12.30–15.30, 19.00–23.00
daily (Aug); closed Jan, Feb & July

La Conchiglia ££ Nestled at the bottom of a long stairway (about
85 steps), overlooking the Bay, La Conchiglia is perfect for a romantic
dinner or a fun lunch. The restaurant also organises pick-ups by boat
from other parts of the island. Be sure to try the special appetiser.
🄰 Spiaggia della Chiaiolella 🄣 (081) 896 7602 🄻 Closed Nov–mid-Apr

La Pergola ££ Advance booking is always recommended at this
intriguing and small garden restaurant, which does wonders with
local ingredients. The menu changes daily and always features a wide
variety of tasty possibilities. 🄰 Via V Rinaldi 37 🄣 (081) 896 9534
🄻 12.30–15.30, 19.00–23.00 Tues–Sun, closed Mon (mid-Apr–July, Sept
& Oct); 12.30–15.30, 19.00–23.00 daily (Aug); closed Nov–mid-Apr

ACCOMMODATION

La Casa sul Mare £–££ This romantic hotel is located in a restored
18th-century *palazzo*. Rooms are air-conditioned and feature beautiful
terraces overlooking the Bay. Transfers to Chiaia beach are available
free of charge. 🄰 Via Salita Castello 13 🄣 (081) 896 8799
🅦 www.lacasasulmare.it

La Tonnara £–££ Families love this property due to its proximity
to a sandy beach. The rooftop and solarium boast stunning
views. 🄰 Via Marina Chiaiolella 51/B 🄣 (081) 810 1052
🅦 www.latonnarahotel.it

🄿 *Procida's colourful harbour*

PRACTICAL
information

Directory

GETTING THERE

By air

For a short stay, those coming from the UK will find flying the quickest and most convenient way to get to Naples. The main entry point is Capodichino airport (see page 48), which is served by most major European airlines and some low-cost services.

Travellers from the USA will need to change planes in a European hub before reaching their final destination, as there are no non-stop services from North America. The average flying time from London is two hours (nine hours from New York), including connections. (See also page 48 for more details on airports.)

Many people are aware that air travel emits CO_2, which contributes to climate change. You may be interested in the possibility of lessening the environmental impact of your flight through **Climate Care**, which offsets your CO_2 emissions by funding environmental projects around the world. Visit  www.jpmorganclimatecare.org

By rail

Though travelling by rail is often a more expensive option than flying from the UK, it at least allows you the chance to see something of the countryside en route. Two of the most common routes by rail either cut through France and into Italy via Turin and Rome or cross through Switzerland and into Italy via Milan.

There are fast and comfortable connections using the French routings from London's St Pancras International station with Eurostar. This option involves a change in Paris, and you may also need to change trains at Milan, Turin or Rome depending on which service you travel on. The total journey time is approximately 20–24 hours,

◐ *A modern tram glides through the old streets of Naples*

depending on connections. The monthly *Thomas Cook European Rail Timetable* has up-to-date schedules for European international and domestic train services.

Eurostar reservations ☎ (UK) 08705 186 186 🌐 www.eurostar.com

Thomas Cook European Rail Timetable ☎ (UK) 01733 416 477; (USA) 1 800 322 3834 🌐 www.thomascookpublishing.com

By road

The Italian motorway system is well integrated into the European motorway network. The easiest motorway to use is the A1, which cuts through Italy and passes through Rome to terminate at Naples. The trip from London via Calais, Paris, Nice, Genoa, Florence and Rome may be picturesque, but it's a long drive at approximately 20 hours.

Driving in Naples is extraordinarily challenging due to the many restrictions to help combat the city's traffic congestion problems and air pollution. If you do decide to drive, try to book into a hotel with parking spots and spend your time either using public transport or walking. Not only will this allow you to see a lot more of the region, but also you'll get around a lot faster and avoid the parking headaches and chaotic driving associated with a stay in the city.

If you happen to break down, national motoring groups (AA or RAC in the UK, and the AAA/CAA in the USA and Canada) have reciprocal agreements with the **Automobile Club d'Italia** (ACI @ Piazzale Tecchio 49D ☎ 803 116 24-hour emergency line 🌐 www.aci.it).

Long-distance buses connect Naples with most other European countries. Most travellers will have to change in Rome to reach their destination. The arrival point is outside the Stazione Centrale. From London by National Express (🌐 www.nationalexpress.com), the fastest journey time is about 30 hours.

By water

More and more cruise ships are including Naples on their itineraries. Cruise ships normally dock at Molo Beverello, from which you are a stone's throw away from all the main sights.

ENTRY FORMALITIES

Visitors to Italy who are citizens of the UK, Ireland, Australia, the USA, Canada or New Zealand will need a passport, but not a visa for stays of up to three months. After that time they must apply for a *permesso di soggiorno* (permit to stay). If you are travelling from other countries, you may need a visa; it is best to check before you leave home.

There are no customs controls at borders for visitors from EU countries. Visitors from EU countries can bring in, or take out, goods without restrictions on quantity or value, as long as these goods are for personal use only. For visitors from outside the EU, most personal effects and the following items are duty-free: one video camera or two still cameras, a portable radio and a laptop computer provided they show signs of use; 400 cigarettes or 50 cigars or 250 g of tobacco; 2 litres of wine or 1 litre of spirits per person over 17 years old; fishing gear; one bicycle; skis; tennis or squash racquets; and golf clubs. As entry requirements and customs regulations are subject to change, you should always check the current situation with your local travel agent, airline or an Italian embassy or consulate before you leave.

MONEY

The currency in Italy is the euro (€). A euro is divided into 100 cents. Notes are in denominations of €5, €10, €20, €50, €100, €200 and €500. Coins are available in denominations of €1 and €2, as well as 1, 2, 5,

10, 20 and 50 cents. You can withdraw money using ATMs at many Italian banks. It is a good idea to use ATM machines located inside the bank, as they are always guarded.

🄘 Many smaller businesses – including some restaurants, taverns, bars, smaller hotels and most market stalls – do not accept credit card payment. This is especially true outside Naples and the main tourist destinations.

HEALTH, SAFETY & CRIME

It is not necessary to take any special health precautions while travelling in Italy. Tap water is safe to drink, but do not drink any water from surrounding lakes or rivers as the region is not known for its commitment to environmentalism. Many Italians prefer bottled mineral water, especially sparkling varieties.

As the region is quite arid and hilly, hiking is a popular pastime. If you do decide to go for a stroll, it is best to inform someone before you embark on your journey as conditions can change fast – especially at the top of Vesuvius. Heatstroke is also a common problem so don't go anywhere without appropriate clothing and ample water supplies.

Pharmacies (*farmacie*) are marked by a large green or red cross. Italian pharmacists can provide informal medical advice on simple ailments. However, prescriptions will always cost more to fill than they would back home.

Italian healthcare is of a good standard, but is not free. Before leaving home, be sure to obtain a European Health Insurance Card (EHIC) to receive any necessary healthcare during a visit to an EU country. The website for ordering a card is 🅦 www.ehic.org.uk; this card replaces the old E111 form. It is also advisable to buy appropriate travel insurance.

Crime has always been a problem in the city of Naples. Its reputation is far worse than reality. Petty theft (bag-snatching, pickpocketing) is the most common form of trouble for tourists and activity is particularly high at the much-frequented historic sights. You are unlikely to experience violence or assault, which occur mainly in the context of gangland activities. Don't carry too much cash and avoid walking around late at night on badly lit streets (especially if you are a woman). Your hotel will warn you about particular areas to avoid.

When using public transport or walking on the street, carry your wallet in your front pocket, keep bags closed at all times, never leave valuables on the ground when you are seated at a table, and always wear camera cases and bags crossed over your chest.

OPENING HOURS

Banks 08.20–13.20, 14.45–15.45 Mon–Fri, closed Sat & Sun
Businesses 09.00–18.00 Mon–Fri, closed Sat & Sun

TOILETS

There are very few public toilet facilities in Naples. The best approach is to use the toilet in a bar. You can usually walk straight in without having to buy a drink. If the bar is empty, it is a matter of politeness to ask the bartender first. Fast-food joints and department stores are other good options if you need a comfort break.

CHILDREN

Naples is generally a child-friendly city. Perfect strangers will dote over your children at every opportunity – but while local kids will often be spotted playing on the streets, your tots may not be as familiar with the rules of the road and will be unused to dealing with speeding Vespas and cars. Don't worry about bringing your children to a restaurant, but don't expect any high chairs or special menus. Luckily, pasta dishes tend to go down well with fussy eaters.

Pompeii (see pages 106–10) makes for a great playground for younger travellers as they can run around and enjoy some freedom while discovering an extraordinary archaeological site. If you want to stay in Naples, the **Città della Scienza** (ⓐ Via Coroglio 104 ⓣ (081) 735 2111 ⓦ www.cittadellascienza.it ⓛ 09.00–17.00 Tues–Sat, 10.00–19.00 Sun, closed Mon ⓘ Admission charge) is a child-friendly science museum and planetarium.

COMMUNICATIONS

Internet

Most Italian phone lines now have sockets for RJ11 jacks, although some older lines will have sockets for large three-pin plugs. Broadband in hotels is still a bit of a luxury, unless you are staying in a major chain property or some of the newer B&Bs. And if you dream of wireless services, dream on. Internet cafés are scattered throughout the city – each one varying in speed. Try to choose a business centre in a hotel or a café with multiple terminals to ensure high-quality service.

Phone

Phone numbers in Naples usually have seven digits. However, older establishments may have only six. All numbers beginning with 800 are toll-free. To use public telephones, buy a card (*scheda telefonica*) from a *tabacchi* (tobacconist's shop), designated by a white capital T on a black background. Hotel telephones usually carry a high surcharge, but not always, so ask at the desk.

Mobile phone numbers begin with 3; if you see an old number with the prefix 03, omit the zero. Your UK, New Zealand and Australian

TELEPHONING NAPLES

Italian phone numbers need to be dialled with their area codes regardless of where you are calling from. All numbers in Naples and its province begin with 081. This includes Sorrento and the islands of Ischia, Capri and Procida. Amalfi and Ravello, located in the province of Salerno, have the code 089. To call from abroad, phone +39 081 or 089, then the individual phone number.

TELEPHONING ABROAD

To make an international call from Naples, dial 00, then the country code (UK = 44, Ireland = 353, USA and Canada = 1, Australia = 61, New Zealand = 64, South Africa = 27) and number, omitting the initial zero in UK numbers.

mobile phone should work in Italy. US and Canadian cell phones may not, so be sure to check with your provider before leaving home.

Public phones in Naples tend to be at busy intersections. As a result, it can be a challenge hearing anything that is being said down the line. The plus side is that almost everyone in Naples has a mobile, so public phone booths are almost always available.

Post

After decades of unreliability, Italy's postal system is really improving. Post boxes are red and have two slots divided between local destinations (*per la città*) and everywhere else (*tutte le altre destinazioni*). Some also have a section with a blue sticker on the front for first-class post. For post being sent out of the country,

The striking central post office building

first class is the only choice you have. First-class service promises 24-hour delivery for any destination in Italy, and three days for anywhere in the EU. For anywhere else in the world, keep your fingers crossed.

Letters less than 20 g to Italy or other EU countries cost 60 cents, or 80 cents to the USA. Australian post costs €1. Registered mail starts at €2.80.

Usual post office opening hours are 08.15–14.30 Monday to Friday and 08.15–12.00 Saturday, closed Sun.

ELECTRICITY

The standard electrical current is 220 volts. Two-pin adaptors can be purchased at most electrical shops.

TRAVELLERS WITH DISABILITIES

For people with severe disabilities such as wheelchair users, Naples is a difficult city to negotiate. Lifts are often too small for a wheelchair to enter and the narrow, cobbled streets can be uncomfortable. Buses are completely wheelchair unfriendly. Try using the modern and efficient metro and overground trains instead. New metro stations have wheelchair-access features (ramps and lifts) incorporated into the design.

In museums, the ground floors are usually accessible, as are those in more modern galleries. Ask staff at the location you are visiting if they can help you, as there may be ramps that can be placed over steps. Often, however, even where ramps exist, you may find them obstructed by cars or motorcycles.

The historic sites of Pompeii (see pages 106–10) and Herculaneum (see page 102), while outdoors, are little better. Access points to the actual collection of ruins have ramps, but the pathways date back to the original Roman period and are littered with wheel ruts and cracks, making manoeuvrability difficult.

Useful organisations for information and advice include:

Ⓦ www.sath.org (USA-based site)

Ⓦ www.access-able.com (general advice on worldwide travel)

Ⓦ http://travel.guardian.co.uk (UK site offering tips and links for travellers with disabilities)

TOURIST INFORMATION

There are tourist offices (EPT) located in Stazione Centrale (Ⓣ (081) 268 779 Ⓛ 09.00–19.00 Mon–Sat, closed Sun) and in Stazione Mergellina (Ⓣ (081) 761 2102 Ⓛ 09.00–14.00 Mon–Sat, closed Sun).

Azienda Autonoma di Soggiorno Cura e Turismo di Napoli (Ⓦ www.inaples.it):

Ⓐ Via San Carlo 9 Ⓣ (081) 402 394

Ⓐ Piazza del Gesù Ⓣ (081) 551 2701

Ⓐ Via Marino Turchi 16 Ⓣ (081) 240 0911

Ⓛ All are open 09.00–13.00, 14.00–18.00 daily

For tourist information in the towns around Naples, see:

Amalfi Ⓦ www.amalfitouristoffice.it

Capri Ⓦ www.capritourism.com or www.capri.net

Ischia and Procida Ⓦ www.infoischiaprocida.it

Pompeii Ⓦ www.pompeiisites.org

Sorrento Ⓦ www.sorrentotourism.com

Vesuvius Ⓦ www.vesuviopark.it

BACKGROUND READING

The Bourbons of Naples by Harold Acton. Good chronicle of the reign of Ferdinand I.

See Naples and Die: The Camorra and Organised Crime by Tom Behan.

A riveting account of the rise of the Camorra clans and their influence in Italian politics and society.

Cosi Fan Tutti by Michael Dibdin. Slick crime novel set in the seedier pockets of Naples featuring detective Aurelio Zen.

Italian Journey by Johann Wolfgang Goethe. Great descriptions of 18th-century Neapolitan life from the German philosopher. There are many versions, but the best features translations by W H Auden.

Pizza Napoletana! by Pamela Sheldon Johns. Everything you ever wanted to know about the history of pizza – and then some. It's worth getting your hands on a copy for the ten authentic pizza recipes from the city's finest establishments.

The Volcano Lover by Susan Sontag. Perfect holiday reading. Romantic, fictional take on the relationship between Lord Nelson and his mistress, Emma Hamilton.

Georgics by Virgil. Classic work written by the ancient historian and poet while living in Naples.

⬭ *Naples, a colourful and vibrant city*

Emergencies

The following are emergency freephone numbers:

Ambulance ❶ 118

Carabinieri (national/military police) ❶ 112

Car breakdown ❶ 803 116

Fire brigade ❶ 115

Polizia di Stato (national police) ❶ 113

MEDICAL SERVICES

If you need a doctor or dentist during your stay, then check out the local English Yellow Pages. The directory will list English-speaking practitioners. If you can't get your hands on this guide, then your hotel concierge and/or the local tourist office should have a list of possibilities.

For emergencies, go directly to the emergency departments of either of the two major hospitals in town (see page 154).

Emergency dentists

Two dentists with English-speaking staff are:

Dottore Federico Lenci ⓐ Via Pontano 7 ❶ (081) 680 650

Dottore Francesco Olivieri ⓐ Via Carducci 6 ❶ (081) 245 7003

Emergency pharmacies

Pharmacies (*farmacie*) are marked by a green or red cross. Over-the-counter medicines are more expensive in Italy than they are in the UK or USA. Most pharmacies keep standard business hours (🕒 08.30–13.00, 16.00–20.00 Mon–Fri and 08.30–13.00 Sat, closed Sun). By law, a sign needs to be posted by the front door pointing customers to the nearest late-opening pharmacy.

◯ *Mounted police in the Centro Storico*

Hospitals

Cardarelli 🅐 Via Cardarelli 9 🕓 (081) 747 1111

Santobono 🅐 Via M Fiore 6 🕓 (081) 220 5355

POLICE

Crimes can be reported to either the Carabinieri or Commissariati. The local police headquarters is **Questura Centrale** (🅐 Via Medina 5 🕓 (081) 794 1111). Prepare to use your patience, as reporting a crime can often be a lengthy process.

If you lose anything or suspect that it has been stolen, then go straight to the nearest police station. While there, you will need to make a *denuncia* (statement). If the loss occurred while on a train, go to the *ufficio oggetti smarriti* (lost property office 🕓 (081) 567 4660) on platform 24 of the Stazione Centrale (see page 52).

Metro thefts and losses need to be reported at the office located at the terminus of the line on which you were travelling. If that's

EMERGENCY PHRASES

Help!	**Fire!**	**Stop!**
Aiuto!	Al fuoco!	Ferma!
Ahyootaw!	*Ahl fooawcaw!*	*Fairmah!*

Call an ambulance/a doctor/the police/the fire service!

Chiamate un'ambulanza/un medico/la polizia/i pompieri!

*Kyahmahteh oon ahmboolahntsa/oon mehdeecaw/
la pawleetsya/ee pompee-ehree!*

impossible, try calling the helpline on ❶ (800) 639 525. The office is open from 08.30–18.00 Mon–Fri. For items left on the SITA bus system, call ❶ (081) 552 2176. Finally, the lost property office at the airport (❶ (081) 789 6237) is open 07.00–24.00 every day.

EMBASSIES & CONSULATES

Australian Embassy ⓐ Via Antonio Bosio 5, Rome ❶ (06) 852 721
Ⓦ www.italy.embassy.gov.au
British Consulate-General ⓐ Via dei Mille 40, Naples
❶ (081) 423 8911 Ⓦ www.britain.it ❶ 09.00–13.30 Mon–Fri,
closed Sat & Sun (times can change in summer)
Canadian Consulate-General ⓐ Via G Carducci 29, Naples
❶ (081) 401 338 ❶ 09.00–13.00 Mon–Fri, closed Sat & Sun
New Zealand Embassy ⓐ Via Zara 28, Rome ❶ (06) 441 7171
Ⓦ www.nzembassy.com
Republic of Ireland Embassy ⓐ Piazza di Campitelli 3, Rome
❶ (06) 697 9121 Ⓦ http://foreignaffairs.gov.ie
Republic of South Africa Embassy ⓐ Via Tanaro 14, Rome
❶ (06) 852 541 Ⓦ www.sudafrica.it
US Consulate-General ⓐ Piazza della Repubblic, Naples
❶ (081) 583 8220 Ⓦ www.naples.usconsulate.gov ❶ 08.00–12.00
Mon–Fri, closed Sat & Sun

ACKNOWLEDGEMENTS

The publishers would like to thank the following individuals and organisations for supplying their copyright photographs for this book: BigStockPhoto.com (Danilo Ascione, pages 40–41 & 141; Pierrette Guertin, page 103); Dreamstime (Andrey Emelyanenko, page 5; Dennis Dolkens, page 21; Chris Sargent, page 36; Pierre Jean Durieu, page 80; Piruso1, page 99; Edwardstaines, page 104; Yuriy Chertok, page 123; Ego04713, page 130; Ronnybas, page 139); iStockphoto.com (tulla, pages 62–3; Giovanni Rinaldi, page 133; Marisa Allegra Williams, page 137); Miami Bar Room/ Benny Galasso, page 97; Petulia Melideo, page 85; Giampiero Monittola, page 90; Caterina Parla, page 57; Anita Theobald, page 26; Neil Setchfield, all others.

Project editor: Jennifer Jahn
Copy editor: Paul Hines
Layout: Donna Pedley
Proofreaders: Kelly Walker & Cath Senker

Send your thoughts to
books@thomascook.com

- Found a great bar, club, shop or must-see sight that we don't feature?

- Like to tip us off about any information that needs a little updating?

- Want to tell us what you love about this handy little guidebook and more importantly how we can make it even handier?

Then here's your chance to tell all! Send us ideas, discoveries and recommendations today and then look out for your valuable input in the next edition of this title.

Email the above address (stating the title) or write to: pocket guides Series Editor, Thomas Cook Publishing, PO Box 227, Coningsby Road, Peterborough PE3 8SB, UK.

WHAT'S IN YOUR GUIDEBOOK?

Independent authors Impartial up-to-date information from our travel experts who meticulously source local knowledge.

Experience Thomas Cook's 165 years in the travel industry and guidebook publishing enriches every word with expertise you can trust.

Travel know-how Thomas Cook has thousands of staff working around the globe, all living and breathing travel.

Editors Travel-publishing professionals, pulling everything together to craft a perfect blend of words, pictures, maps and design.

You, the traveller We deliver a practical, no-nonsense approach to information, geared to how you really use it.

Useful phrases

English	Italian	Approx pronunciation
BASICS		
Yes	Sì	*See*
No	No	*Noh*
Please	Per favore	*Pehr fahvohreh*
Thank you	Grazie	*Grahtsyeh*
Hello	Buongiorno/Ciao	*Bwonjohrnoh/Chow*
Goodbye	Arrivederci/Ciao	*Ahreevehderchee/Chow*
Excuse me	Scusi	*Skoozee*
Sorry	Mi dispiace	*Mee deespyahcheh*
That's okay	Va bene	*Vah behneh*
I don't speak Italian	Non parlo italiano	*Non pahrloh eetahlyahnoh*
Do you speak English?	Parla inglese?	*Pahrlah eenglehzeh?*
Good morning	Buongiorno	*Bwonjohrnoh*
Good afternoon	Buon pomeriggio	*Bwon pohmehreejoh*
Good evening	Buona sera	*Bwonah sehrah*
Goodnight	Buona notte	*Bwonah nohteh*
My name is ...	Mi chiamo ...	*Mee kyahmoh ...*
NUMBERS		
One	Uno	*Oonoh*
Two	Due	*Dooeh*
Three	Tre	*Treh*
Four	Quattro	*Kwahttroh*
Five	Cinque	*Cheenkweh*
Six	Sei	*Say*
Seven	Sette	*Sehteh*
Eight	Otto	*Ohtoh*
Nine	Nove	*Nohveh*
Ten	Dieci	*Dyehchee*
Twenty	Venti	*Ventee*
Fifty	Cinquanta	*Cheenkwahntah*
One hundred	Cento	*Chentoh*
SIGNS & NOTICES		
Airport	Aeroporto	*Ahehrohpohrtoh*
Railway station	Stazione ferroviaria	*Statsyoneh fehrohveeahreeyah*
Platform	Binario	*Beenahreeyoh*
Smoking/non-smoking	Fumatori/non fumatori	*Foomahtohree/non foomahtohree*
Toilets	Bagni	*Bahnyee*
Ladies/Gentlemen	Signore/Signori	*Seenyoreh/Seenyohree*
Subway	Metropolitana	*Mehtrohpohleetahnah*